8-16-00

Obsessions Die Hard

Motorcycling the Pan American Highway's Jungle Gap

May peace be with you through all the journeys yet to come

Jesse,

D0097293

"Incredible Journeys" Books
Available from Whitehorse Press

The Endless Ride
Investment Biker
Jupiter's Travels
The Motorcycle Diaries: A Journey Around So. America
Obsessions Die Hard
One Man Caravan
Riding the Edge
Two Wheels to Adventure
Two Wheels to Panama
Zen and the Art of Motorcycle Maintenance

Obsessions Die Hard

Motorcycling the Pan American Highway's Jungle Gap

Ed Culberson

Whitehorse Press
North Conway, New Hampshire

Copyright © 1991 and 1996 by Ed Culberson

All rights reserved. No part of this publication
may be reproduced or transmitted in any form or
by any means, electronic or mechanical, including
photocopy, recording, or any information storage
or retrieval system, without permission in
writing from the publisher.

Photographs are by the author.

We recognize that some words, model names and
designations mentioned herein are the property
of the trademark holder. We use them for
identification purposes only.

An Incredible Journeys Book.
Published August 1996 by
   Whitehorse Press
   3424 North Main Street - P.O. Box 60
   North Conway, New Hampshire 03860 U.S.A.
   Phone: 603-356-6556 or 800-531-1133
   FAX: 603-356-6590
   E-mail:75030.2554@compuserve.com

Whitehorse Press is a trademark of
Kennedy Associates.

ISBN 1-884313-06-X

5 4 3 2

Printed in the United States of America

Dedication

Obsessions *Die Hard* is a modest tribute to the men whose endeavors over the past seven decades have created the Pan American Highway System — the world's most extensive road network.

Few of the highway's daily users — the millions of drivers, riders, passengers, hitchhikers, pedestrians and workers — ever consider what the road is or how it came to be. Nor are they aware of or concerned about the visionaries, statesmen, engineers and builders, many of whom dedicated their careers and lives to the hemispheric project.

But there are others who have developed an abiding appreciation for what the road represents. For them, the Pan American Highway is a living, dynamic, ever-changing route to adventure — a destination in and of itself.

I am one of them, and this book is my eulogy to the architects and artisans of the road. It is also a special accolade to the *Darienistas,* that resolute group who infused me with my own version of their obsession.

Contents

List of Maps

PRAISE FOR *OBSESSIONS DIE HARD*

"I heard that Culberson had done it. Cut the Gordian Knot, squared the circle, ridden his damned gap. Bugs, leeches, caimans, Manuel Noriega, and fried BMW diode boards, oh my!"
— Dr. Robert Hellman, Editor, *On the Level*
BMW Riders Association International

"This is an old-fashioned adventure story from the man who invented the whole category of Adventure Touring in this hemisphere. The style is fluid (and) the story compelling . . ."
— BMW Riders Association

"The wildest trip I've ever read about. It's an incredible story. It's a great story. Full of adventure and a lot of agony. This is absolutely never-put-it-down reading."
— Clive Thomas, WWNZ-AM

"An inspiring story of how determination can overcome adversity and failure. Culberson traveled an area so inhospitable that a myth about its impenetrability has evolved over the centuries . . . but the gap didn't stop Ed Culberson's dream. It turned into an obsession."

— *hack'd*

"A riveting account of Culberson's unusual trek through the Darien jungle. I recommend it, unreservedly, to anyone interested in reading an extremely well-written, true adventure story."

— *Panama Canal Record*

"Culberson's narrative is especially interesting because it's incredible that both man and machine could survive a journey of such tortuous dimensions. His story is an impressive record of human grit."

— *Rider Magazine*

1

The Myth and the Curse

*Contemporary man has rationalized myths,
but has not been able to destroy them.*

Octavio Paz
The Labyrinth of Solitude

"Whaddya mean there ain't no road?" protested the scruffy, bearded man on the mud-encrusted, enduro-style motorcycle with a barely legible California license plate.

The biker had pulled up beside me to ask directions as I was getting ready to mount my motorcycle at Stevens Circle in Balboa, on the Pacific side of the Panama Canal. It was 1974 and he had just arrived from the United States. From the looks of both bike and rider, he had taken a severe beating on the four-thousand-mile ride down to the Canal Zone.

"But dammit, the map shows a road running all the way from here to Colombia!"

He thrust a tattered oil company map at me and pointed indignantly to the dashed line of the Pan American Highway running east from Panama City before curving southward to the Colombian border and beyond.

"You're right," I conceded, "but that's the *proposed* route. As of now, the road ends about fifty miles from here. Beyond the Chagres and Bayano rivers there's nothing but the jungles and swamps of the Darien region. It would take a small army to get you and your motorcycle through the next 150 miles."

You poor bastard, I mused. Here you've busted your tail riding all the way down through Mexico, Central America and half of Panama, only to bump up against a roadblock you didn't even know existed.

"So how in hell do I get to South America?"

"Well, you could put your bike on board a ship over there at Pier 18," I said, pointing to the Panama Canal Balboa harbor only a block away. "Or you can fly it out to Colombia on a cargo aircraft from Tocumen Airport on the other side of Panama City. Either way, it will take time and cost you a bundle of money."

Although I didn't realize it, my advice was helping to perpetuate a myth, a centuries-old belief that it was simply not possible for outsiders, no matter how intrepid, to venture through eastern Panama's Darien region and the area surrounding the Atrato River in Colombia.

I knew little then of the myth, but it didn't matter. The battered biker didn't look like he needed any more bad news. Thoroughly discouraged, he muttered a word of thanks, kick-started his bike to a sputtering rumble and slowly rode off around the circle.

I never saw the Californian again and do not know if he ever pressed on to the south. But that same scene, with minor variations in vehicles, characters and dialogue, has been replayed many times over the years.

Scores of unknowing travelers — motorists, motorcycle riders, bicyclists and backpackers — have journeyed south to Panama or north to Colombia expecting the Pan American Highway to give them an open passage across the border between the two countries. But they have been disheartened to find that along the narrow isthmus there is still a break in the highway that is supposed to extend all the way between Alaska and Argentina. That obstruction, known as the Darien Gap — in Spanish *el Tapón del Darién,* The Stopper — has sustained its myth by proving to be a nearly impassable barrier for wayfarers.

Today, adventuresome travelers can head east from Panama City by bumping along the 180 miles of mostly unpaved road that has been slowly and crudely extended into the previously isolated Darien region. But at the decrepit village of Yaviza the road runs out. The rutted dirt track stops at the banks of the Chucunaque River and does not begin again until the far side of the Atrato River in Colombia, a gap of less than 100 miles. When it does pick up again, portions of the route to

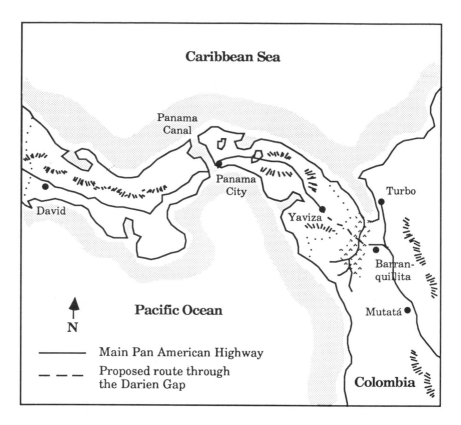

Republic of Panama

Bogotá are often blocked by flooding, landslides and massive rebuilding projects.

The gap in the Pan American Highway isn't much in terms of the sixteen-thousand-mile-long main route, which runs through eighteen countries and spans over one-half the circumference of the earth. And there is still another thirty-thousand miles of alternate and secondary roads that are also part of the overall Pan American Highway System.

Most travelers between the northern and southern hemispheres usually bridge the Darien Gap by flying over it or boating around it. But for hard-core wayfarers intent on covering the entire primary route between Alaska and Argentina by land, that short, obscure stretch where there is no road of any kind is a frustrating obstacle, as the California biker discovered.

A decade after our brief encounter in Balboa, I would challenge that barrier. I wanted to ride my motorcycle the full length of the main Pan American Highway between Fairbanks and Buenos Aires. My goal was to cover every mile of the established road and somehow make my way through the proposed route in the Darien. Nobody, as far as I could determine, had ever taken a motorcycle through the gap by that route. I thought of it as the Mount Everest of motorcycling.

This scheme would open up to me an entirely new spectrum of adventuring. Heretofore, most of my land travels had been relatively straightforward — by car, often with family and usually on the most-travelled roads. Even my motorcycling escapades had been limited to manageable risks along reasonable routes, such as cycling U.S. Route 1 from Florida to Maine. But this was a far more dangerous game, one which went well beyond my youthful dreams of sedately touring down the Pan American Highway — an idea which began during my high school days in Washington, D.C., where I was born and raised.

I could clearly recall my tenth-grade geography teacher, Mrs. Hanft, who was piously strict, yet compassionate, in making her dreaded semester-long study assignments.

"And you, Edwin," she said, "will make a report on the Pan American Highway. We must remember that this remarkable cooperative effort with our Latin neighbors has been a major part of President Franklin Delano Roosevelt's Good Neighbor Policy."

"Yes, Ma'am," I said dutifully. I strongly suspected that Mrs. Hanft had given me this topic because she knew I played softball on the Ellipse, a park just down from the White House and across 17th Street from the Pan American Union headquarters where the Pan Am highway project had been organized. In those more trusting times I could wander freely around that ornately marbeled building to monitor the progress of the faraway road-building project that was intended to connect all the major capitals of the Western Hemisphere. This channeling of teenage interest subtly directed my thoughts and desires to travel, especially in Latin America, and to venture along the Pan American Highway.

But thirty-five years later my involvement with the Pan American Highway began to focus on the Darien Gap itself. I had returned to Panama by motorcycle, on my way to ride the Pan Am through South America. There I was confronted with the same dilemma the California biker had encountered six years earlier. I could not penetrate the Darien's green barrier of rain forest, jungle and swamp. I had to dodge around it by air and sea to get to Cape Horn and back.

This detour was a frustration that churned away inside me, only to mushroom into a full-blown obsession. Sooner or later, someone was going to ride a motorcycle the entire length of the Pan Am — and get through the gap on the way. Who better to do it than me? It might be my last chance to earn some sort of recognition in a world where there was hardly a spot remaining that had not already been discovered, explored and exploited.

The myth also nagged at me. I would be challenging the centuries-old tradition that the Darien region was impenetrable to outsiders. I could readily understand how the Darien's reputation started and why the legend persisted for so long. For centuries Darien adventurers had encountered a combination of oppressive climate, tropical diseases, abominable topography and unfriendly inhabitants — both human and animal. The mixture often proved deadly and many did not survive.

Vasco Nuñez de Balboa fathered the myth, which discouraged any meaningful exploration ever since the Spaniard marched across the Isthmus of Panama to discover the Pacific Ocean in 1513. Even large-scale incursions could not dent the region's invincibility. The Darien mercilessly decimated a colony of Scots founded in 1698 at Calidonia Bay on the Atlantic side of the isthmus.

Through the centuries, however, the outside world gnawed away at the Darien's perimeter. The search for an isthmian canal route in the mid-1800s brought in crews of explorers and surveyors, some with hugely creative imaginations. An Irish physician and member of the Royal Geographic Society, Dr. Edward Cullen, claimed to have walked over a trail through the Darien whose elevation was no more than 150 feet above sea level. Cullen's report caused an immediate uproar and sparked spirited debates in all the major geographic societies. But Cullen turned out to be a charlatan, although a century and a half later I would wish that he had been right as I sweated mightily to push, drag and winch my motorcycle over sharp ridges and steeply rising hills hundreds of feet higher than Cullen had described.

Before being proved false, Cullen's account led to tragic explorations of the Darien. U.S. Navy Lieutenant Isaac Strain undertook one such expedition in 1854. He led a group of twenty-seven men ashore at Aclá, near Calidonia Bay, expecting to follow Cullen's easy trail. Strain quickly became disoriented and refused to follow the directions of Indians whom he thought were trying to mislead him. He wandered for the next forty-nine days along the Chucunaque River before reaching a settlement on the Pacific side. During the trek, seven sailors perished from sickness and starvation. Strain himself had wasted to seventy-five pounds.

The desolation and fearful terrain of Panama's eastern region helped persuade the celebrated Frenchman Ferdinand de Lesseps to do his canal-building work on the narrowest part of the isthmus. He dug parallel to the Las Cruces trail, a route used by the Spanish *conquistadores* and in the mid-1800s by would-be prospectors en route to the California gold fields.

After the United States took over the project and completed the canal in 1914, commercial development took root and Panama's growth focused around the canal. Once the deadly tropical diseases of yellow fever, cholera and malaria were brought under control, adventurers took a bolder attitude toward exploring the isolated regions west and east of the canal, including the Darien.

World War II also spurred the parting of the verdant green curtain obscuring Panama's interior. Coastal roads were hurriedly extended outward from the canal, and the port cities at the entrances to the waterway were linked by a transverse route, the Boyd-Roosevelt Highway. Ground forces made exploratory forays into the jungle areas, and airfields for anti-submarine patrol planes were hastily laid out along the coastlines. The military even built an airstrip in the Darien.

The Pan American Highway project helped push back Panama's jungles and also took direct aim at the Darien. Ever since the concept of building the world's longest highway system was first developed in 1923, the plan called for a road to be built through the Darien region. The Organization of American States, successor to the Pan American Union, accelerated the work in the post-war years, sponsoring a relentless extension of the Pan Am from each side of the Darien. The OAS succeeded in narrowing the gap to what seemed to be an almost minor impediment to a final link-up.

The OAS appointed a Darien Gap subcommittee to oversee completion of this last, symbolic section of roadway. As a result, this part of the Pan American Highway project developed a unique, multi-national character and involved a cast of players who were unlike their lesser-known counterparts working on more routine sections of the highway.

The Pan Am has been a decades-long, plodding endeavor that has never produced any heroes on the scale of the revered canal-builders, rapacious railroad barons or flamboyant airline developers. With little glamor and little capacity to excite the public, the project has never been a path to glory for any of its dedicated workers. Many people have never even heard of the Pan American Highway, much less sung praises to its creators.

But members of the Darien Gap subcommittee, or *Darienistas* as they proudly called themselves, did achieve some fame, and even a touch of notoriety. In the 1950s and 60s they boldly mixed politics with ordinary engineering decisions and argued heatedly over the exact route to be followed to satisfy widely divergent Panamanian and Colombian self-interests.

Jose J. March, a highly-respected Mexican engineer, was one of the most ardent *Darienistas*. He readily saw the so-called Myth of the Darien as a well-entrenched opponent and attacked it directly, even preparing an epitaph for the time when the long-standing folk tale would finally be dispatched. March wrote a book, *El Mito del Darién (The Myth of the Darien),* in which he called for the official demise of the myth.

In 1960, a motor vehicle expedition set out to challenge the Darien and its myth. Members of the expedition, which was jointly sponsored by the OAS and the National Geographic Society, survived four months and twenty days of horrendous physical privations and punishing trail-cutting labors to break through the gap. The weary crews and their battered jeep and Land Rover followed the proposed route of the Pan Am to the Colombian border at Palo de las Letras, a small monument in an uninhabited area that marks the border. The exhausted expeditioners struggled to reach the Atrato River, where the group with the jeep floated downriver to the coast and on to the Caribbean port of Turbo, Colombia, to return to Panama. The Land Rover and its crew headed upriver to Quibdó, Colombia, there to pick up the road to Bogotá.

Although the expeditioners had not stayed on the proposed track of the Pan Am east of the Atrato, March claimed the myth had been destroyed. He considered the expedition proof that the Pan Am's proposed route through the Darien was feasible. March maintained that a massive construction effort could produce an all-weather road through the Darien that would be the final step in completing the Pan American Highway.

Despite March's unbridled optimism, the Darien Gap has not yet been closed, and remnants of the myth still exist. If the noted Mexican poet and philosopher Octavio Paz is correct, the Myth of the Darien may be one of those which has not been destroyed but rather rationalized.

Some observers claim that the Myth of the Darien may have been transformed into something more sinister — the Curse of the Darien. A far more private threat than the myth, the curse is directed at the individual, the person who dares challenge the Darien and its ancient protective barriers.

The Darien's history is replete with examples to foster such an idea. Balboa, on his return to the Darien, was beheaded by a treacherous subordinate. Lt. Strain never recovered from his Darien ordeal and died several years later. More recently, several of the most active *Darienistas* have succumbed. Jose March met an untimely death, and Tomas Guardia, Junior, a dedicated Panamanian leader of the Darien Gap subcommittee and veteran of the 1960 expedition, died of what the authorities listed as only a medically undefinable "Darien disease."

These stories did not overly concern me in 1985 as I was preparing to make my first attempt at the gap. Not being superstitious, I did not really care whether the myth had been destroyed or transformed into some sort of curse, or even if it existed at all. I could not afford to worry over vague tales of how Darien Gappers had been struck down in retribution for their trespassing.

I was far more concerned with pitting my middle-age endurance against the tangible physical dangers. I would be entering an isolated region where some of the world's heaviest rainfall occurs. I would have only a two-month window of weather dry enough to complete the passage through the Darien Gap. I would have to contend with dense tropical rain forests, jagged terrain and, once across the border and into Colombia, the trackless jungle and miasmal swamps guarding the Atrato River basin.

The trek would demand that I carefully conserve my strength, supplies and fuel. I would have to devise a scheme to survive and move about with the burden of the motorcycle in an environment about which I had studied intently, but only from a respectful distance.

These were my real concerns, the natural barriers

that had helped perpetuate the myth and had given rise to the curse. I believed I could overcome these hurdles with forethought, perseverance and determination. The physical rigors were the price I was willing to pay for almost a lifetime of hopes and dreams, of a fascination with a highway and an obsession to travel it as no one had ever done before.

2

Planting the Seed

I am fevered with the sunset,
I am fretful with the bay,
For the wander-thirst is on me,
And my soul is in Cathay

Richard Hovey
The Sea Gypsy

My juvenile love affair with the Pan American Highway turned to early estrangement when I went off to college and then rashly joined the Army at the outbreak of the Korean War. I had been too young for the Big War, and Korea seemed to be my chance to salvage a little residual martial glory. My enlistment also turned out to be a providential move. Twenty years later it would put me on the Pan American Highway heading south.

I survived Korea and stayed in the Army, eventually becoming an intelligence officer. In preparation for an assignment in the Panama Canal Zone, I underwent intensive Spanish language training, and I gladly obeyed orders to become intimately familiar with Latin America. But before the Army could send me to Panama, the Cuban missile crisis and then the Vietnam War intervened to send me off to far places well beyond the Latin world.

After an eight-year delay, the Army made good the promise to send me to the Canal Zone. Elated with the orders, I immediately contacted the travel officer.

"Can I drive my car to Panama?" I asked.

I expected an administrative knee-jerk reaction — of course you can't. But the man said, "Well, if you want to risk it, and there's nothing in the regulations to say you can't, then I guess you can."

I could, and I did. In 1971 I joyfully made my first journey down the Pan American Highway. In the company of my two teenage daughters I left Florida for Panama driving a stodgy Volkswagen station wagon.

We had a slow-paced ride, feeling our way down the narrow, winding, usually two-lane asphalt roads that were mindful of 1940s back-country roads in the United States. We took a week to get through Mexico, and then a day each to travel between the Central American capitals of Guatemala City, San Salvador and Managua in Nicaragua. We were traveling along the part of the Pan Am officially known as the Inter-American Highway.

After we crawled up and over the cloud-shrouded Hill of Death in Costa Rica — the highest point on the entire Pan American Highway System — we encountered the last stretch of still-unfinished road north of the Panama Canal. For the next 160 miles we bumped and slammed over the rock-strewn roadbed. We prayed for the sight of each new concrete bridge that would give us a few yards of respite from the terrible beating that we and the Volkswagen were taking.

Crossing the border into Panama was our salvation, and we gratefully rolled along a paved road toward the Chiriquí province capital of David. Perhaps relieved that the rough road was behind us, my oldest daughter, Dorothy, marveled, "Gee, Dad, we've been on the road for two weeks now and have gone over four thousand miles without having a single problem."

At that moment the overloaded station wagon's rear end started to sway as a rear tire went flat — a belated victim of the abominable Costa Rican roadway. After I peevishly ordered Dorothy to record the moment by camera, I sweated in the bright tropical sunlight to change the badly mangled tire.

We overnighted in David and then drove eastward along a broad, concrete highway to the Canal Zone. We were now following one of the newest and best-engineered stretches of the Pan Am. Panama had agreed to pay a premium on top of its share of the cost if the United States and the OAS would approve using more-expensive concrete instead of asphalt. As a result, the route is one of the Pan Am's longest runs of concrete highway.

While we were making the road trip, my wife and

two younger daughters had flown to Panama where we rendezvoused in the Canal Zone to begin four years of tranquility and excitement, of purpose and pleasure.

At that time the Canal Zone was renowned — some said notorious — for its peculiar insularity.

"It's the only real American colony left," boasted one Zonian, a proud third-generation Panama Canal Company employee.

"It's the only purely socialistic society in the free world," said another more pragmatic resident. "Where else is the size of your living quarters determined by your job assignment and all the other essential services provided by Big Daddy?"

My family and I were able to share the dual benefits of life in the military community and the parallel society created and controlled by the Panama Canal Company. I enjoyed living adjacent to the canal. In addition to the neat, orderly, predictable and secure life in the zone, there was the daily excitement of living at THE FUNNEL FOR WORLD COMMERCE as Canal Zone vehicle license plates proclaimed.

I commuted to my duty station by crossing over the sweeping arch of the Bridge of the Americas, from which I could watch the never-ending procession of ships moving along the channel between the Pacific anchorage and the Miraflores and Pedro Miguel locks. The ships and the canal stimulated a continuous enthusiasm in me, as if I had surrogate access to the entire world.

Not all my experiences were as rewarding, however. My job assignment had me working in the "Tunnel" — a concrete-lined shaft bored into the rock monolith of Ancon Hill which dominates, Gibraltar-like, the entire Pacific approach to the canal. The Tunnel was a windowless dungeon with dank air and a disturbing isolation from the bright, green tropical world outside.

Some workers found the constricting tunnel corridor brought on tremors of claustrophobia. The Tunnel gave me occasional flashbacks to my earlier career as a tank commander, riding into combat with the hatches buttoned up and at the mercy of unseen enemies skulking around outside. No amount of off-duty running or racketball could offset the suffocating atmosphere of the Tunnel.

Is it any wonder that when I had to find an alternate means of commuting across the canal — my wife having commandeered the Volkswagen — that I selected one of the freest, most liberating modes of land transport available? I decided to buy a motorcycle.

The decision was also tempered with a heavy dose of practicality. Americans did not have to pay the stiff Panamanian import duties, so I could buy a new motorcycle cheaply. And I assessed the risks of riding in the well-regulated traffic of the Canal Zone as relatively low.

I did have one disturbing question. In an era when the manufacturer was claiming that "you meet the nicest people on a Honda," how would my fellow officers view me on a still-less-than-socially-acceptable vehicle, even one so sedate as a little 125-cc machine? This was a major concern, because I was known as a straight arrow — an unswerving believer in high discipline and good order. But I came to terms with the question by simply saying, "Screw it! I'm going to ride a motorcycle."

Life on the bike began fitfully. I had to teach myself

how to manage the toy-like single-cylinder machine, and I was glad to have started out small, unwittingly following the pattern of most motorcyclists. The little red bike was a very forgiving learning tool as I coaxed it up and over the Bridge of the Americas several times a day.

My infatuation with the bike grew as fresh panoramas of travel opened up to me. I covered the entire Canal Zone on that faithful Honda. But as my skills increased I found the bike and its small engine hard put to keep out of the way of the racketing buses and careening taxis on the steep grades of the bridge and the surrounding hills. So I traded the 125 for a 350-cc bike, a dual-purpose machine designed for hardier riding on or off the road. The upswept mufflers and high exhaust pipes gave it an enduro look, and the ride, even on smooth surfaces, was bone jarring. But this was of little concern to my still-uncritical cycling senses, and I rode the 350 for thousands of memorable miles around the Canal Zone and out into the hinterlands of Panama.

By now I had become addicted to biking. It rekindled my desire to travel almost indiscriminately. Yet later I developed a purpose — a personal goal to ride every mile of paved road in the Republic of Panama.

The incentives were many. Much as I enjoyed the comfort and orderliness of the Canal Zone, the real Panama lay beyond the confines of the ten-mile-wide strip running alongside the canal. The zone was like a U.S.-Mexican border town. Only well away from the border do the local attitudes and actions towards gringos change, softening and mellowing with each mile beyond the frontier. I wanted to sample a more genuine Panamanian atmosphere. And I wanted to practice my Spanish — which I seldom needed in the Canal Zone — while searching out Panamanian history and discovering the geographic influences that have made the isthmus so important.

I also justified the travel professionally. As an intelligence officer, I had been tasked to become well versed in the area — to understand the people and the events that were daily reported to the four-star commander and his staff. During this time, the early seventies, American-Panamanian conflicts were infrequent. General Omar Torrijos, Panama's leader, had muted anti-American feelings remaining after the violent 1964 riots. The general was also taking a rational approach to working out treaties for the eventual elimination of the Canal Zone and the turnover of the canal to the Panamanians. Even so, the U.S. Southern Command saw a continuing need to collect information and photographs of key areas and sites. And I was able to respond, using the motorcycle as my transport. The bike also provided a rather disarming means of masking my official activities. After all, who would expect a gringo spy in Panama to ride around on a motorcycle?

The Pan American Highway was my main beat, simply because it is the only east-west route on the Isthmus of Panama. West of the canal, which actually runs more north and south due to the bend in the isthmus, lies the *Cordillera Central,* a spine-like range of mountains running along the center of the country. The cordillera sets up a coastal corridor route for the Pan Am on the Pacific side. East of the canal, a central valley between coastal ranges of hills makes the interior the most logical path for the Pan Am leading into the Darien region.

"Well, where are you off to now?" would become a frequent question as I turned my off-duty time into a series of excursions that almost wore out the 350-cc bike. So I moved up to a Honda 500 — a new four-cylinder, mid-size touring machine far better suited to my increasingly longer travels. By now the Pan American Highway had been paved all the way between Panama and San Jose, Costa Rica, which meant I could reach the heights of the Hill of Death in comfort.

I also made excursions eastward, along a recently constructed section of the Pan American Highway extending beyond Tocumen Airport. I would leave the highway and ride up into the hills that spawned the headwaters of the Chagres River, which fed the Panama Canal locks, or ride farther east to the Bayano River near where the inhospitable Darien region began. Sometimes I would ride alone to photograph the construction of a dam on the Bayano. Other times I rode out with groups of bikers to explore the end of the highway at the site of a new bridge over the Bayano.

A year later I traded bikes again. I had received orders to attend a school in Washington, D.C., and I used the trip to buy my first BMW motorcycle and ride it back to Panama. The forty-eight-hundred-mile trip was a resounding success — I had found the perfect mount to match the road. The riding was euphoric, despite the onset of the Central American rainy season. The roads over which my daughters and I had bounced and rattled three years before were much improved. I was glad to see that on the existing Pan Am routes maintenance and improvement appeared to be an on-going process.

Back in Panama, I had been released from the dark

confines of the Tunnel and promoted to a job in an office with windows that let the bright tropic sun constantly beckon. And my new motorcycle was an irresistible inducement to continue touring. I often headed eastward out to the end of the Pan Am to gingerly walk across the nearly completed steel skeleton of the Bayano River bridge which pointed to the still-inaccessible Darien. I also kept cruising the familiar highway westward to Chiriquí province and to Costa Rica.

The black BMW soon became well-known, due in part to its distinctive license plate. In the Canal Zone it was customary to assign the first numbered vehicle tags to the governor, a U.S. Army Corps of Engineers Major General who was the titular head of the Panama Canal Company. But he did not have a motorcycle, so I inherited a prestigious M-1 Canal Zone license plate. The tag became a constant source of wonder to those who were never sure just who the helmeted rider was. The governor? The president, perhaps? Or maybe even *el comandante!*

In January 1975 I took off westward for the cordillera with a fellow officer-cyclist. I had heard of an isolated area in Costa Rica adjacent to the Panamanian border in which blue-eyed, blond-haired immigrants from post-war Europe had established a wine-growing colony. Curious about the reports, we headed for the border — but not via the Pan American Highway. Instead, we tried to cross by picking our way along a little-known upland route. But we were turned back by suspicious Panamanian border guards for failing to have the proper documentation.

Still determined to check out the European settlement, I chose another approach. I asked our liaison agent to get advance approval to cross the border from the *Guardia Nacional,* the combined police and military forces of Panama. And who better to provide me with the permission than the head of the GN's intelligence and security service, Lieutenant Colonel Manuel Antonio Noriega.

I had once met Noriega, who was, in some respects, both a counterpart and a competitor. I knew he could issue travel papers to which his guards on the Costa Rican border would instantly respond. Not just because of his rank and position, but because in Chiriquí province some considered Noriega a hero.

In 1968, then-Lieutenant Noriega seized the radio station in David in support of a coup launched by General Torrijos. The general and several colonels had wrested power from a newly elected civilian government. The grateful Torrijos immediately promoted Noriega to major and made him zone commander of Chiriquí province — the most sought-after post in the Guardia Nacional outside of the Panamanian capital.

A year later, in 1969, Noriega again showed his loyalty to Torrijos. While the general was vacationing in Mexico City, less-than-loyal cohorts back in Panama quietly pulled off a bloodless palace coup. Following the tradition of most Panamanian government upheavals, the rebellious colonels wired Torrijos not to return.

The furious Torrijos was unable to book a commercial flight back to Panama. So he hired an itinerant American pilot and his small, single-engine plane and barnstormed back to Panama through Central America. Night had fallen when the plane sputtered across the border into Panama, and the only nearby airstrip was an unlighted field on the outskirts of David.

The resourceful Torrijos radioed ahead to Noriega for help. Noriega quickly commandeered military and civilian vehicles in the area, some at gunpoint. He deployed the vehicles so their headlights shone along the airstrip, lighting the way for the aircraft's perilous landing.

Noriega then led the convoy that carried Torrijos triumphantly along the Pan American Highway to Panama City. After the rebel colonels recovered from their surprise, they hurriedly removed themselves from the scene. (The colonels were lucky. Twenty years later Noriega would abrogate the usual Panamanian convention of allowing coup losers to escape to a sanctuary when he summarily executed Major Moises Giroldi and his would-be rebels.)

Torrijos rewarded Noriega this time with a promotion to lieutenant colonel. He also kept Noriega in Panama City and made him chief of all the security forces in Panama — a post eminently suited to the crafty man.

The GN troops in Chiriquí would pay heed to anything endorsed by Noriega, so I had the liaison agent request a letter from him endorsing my travels. I knew my next jaunt through Chiriquí and the cordillera to the European settlement in Costa Rica would succeed when I received what is called with morbid humor a "don't shoot him" letter signed by Noriega. It was written on the letterhead of the Guardia Nacional G-2, the intelligence and security service, and addressed in Spanish: "To Whom It May Concern." The letter requested that both the Panamanian and Costa Rican authorities assist me in my travels through the border areas.

I traveled alone on this trip, and the Noriega letter easily got me across the border. I found the rumors of the settlers were true. They had come from Germany, Switzerland and northern Italy. Although their efforts to grow grapes for wine had failed, they had turned to other creative agricultural projects and were doing quite well growing hops, flowers and exotic vegetables.

I returned to the Pan American Highway in Costa Rica and headed back to Panama. My showing up on the Costa Rican side of the border turned out to be a surprise to the Panamanian customs and immigration officials. They could not believe that I had made the mountainous circuit by motorcycle, and by myself.

"Our records and your passport do not show that you left Panama. So how can you return?" the head of the immigration office asked.

"Easily," I said with a confident smile, showing him the letter from his former zone commander.

The Noriega letter and the M-1 license plate quickly dispelled his suspicions and got me readmitted without even going through the usual niggling formalities. It was a valuable lesson in travel tactics which I would draw upon again ten years later.

Much as I was attracted by the far more accessible and scenic western provinces, the lure of the eastern end of Panama was becoming equally strong. I kept bumping into reminders that the Pan American Highway stopped less than a day's ride east from Balboa. On frequent flights out to Contadora Island in the Gulf of Panama, and across the isthmus to the San Blas islands on the Atlantic coast, I could occasionally see through the cloud blanket of the Darien's nine-to-ten-month rainy season.

The red track of the road was slowly being extended past the Bayano. But near Cañazas, the rough gravel and dirt road was stopped by a green wall of jungle and the rumpled terrain of the *Comarca de San Blas* — an autonomous district controlled by the Indians.

Even though the OAS *Darienistas* and the Republic of Panama engineers were working hard to carve through the wilderness, the barely upgraded trail did nothing to help travelers get through the rest of the gap. And while many turned back at the prospect, assorted adventurers using a mix of motor vehicles did attempt passage through the Darien.

Prowling about the shelves of the Panama Canal Company library, I learned of U.S. Army forays over the years and avidly read of the 1960 OAS-National Geographic Society expedition to the Colombian border. I also found an incredible story of a failed expedition made up of Chevrolet Corvairs which were driven into the Darien as a General Motors Corporation publicity stunt back when the rear-engine car was introduced.

In late 1971 and early 1972 I followed closely the ordeal of a British expedition led by Major John Blashford-Snell. The expedition's experiences are documented in Russell Braddon's book *The Hundred Days of Darien*.

The indefatigable Blashford-Snell and his intrepid group of soldiers and civilians managed to winch, push and drag their Land Rover and Range Rover vehicles through the Darien. They were the first adventurers to follow the entire proposed route of the Pan American Highway to where the road started again at its northern terminus in Barranquillita, Colombia. But they suffered casualties and courted disaster every step of the way.

I also read local newspaper reports of a Panama Canal Company employee named Bob Webb who in 1972 set out for Colombia on a Rokon dual-drive motorcycle, only to fail within days after his start. Not daunted, he rode back to the Darien the next year in company with a fellow canal company employee, Ron Merrill. They managed to get their rough-terrain Rokons two-thirds of the way to the border before having to abandon them.

Despite their setbacks, Webb and Merrill returned on foot the following dry season, resurrected their bikes and pressed on across the border to the Rio Cacarica. They used canoes on the Cacarica to reach the Atrato River. But there they left the proposed route of the Pan American Highway and floated downriver to the Caribbean and on to Turbo before returning to Panama by boat.

These accounts fascinated me. But as I read them I was thinking far beyond the Darien barrier. The rest of the Pan American Highway in South America had become the attraction. I started to think about getting the BMW over or around the gap and touring the Pan Am in the Southern Hemisphere.

But before I could put the idea into action, I had to take a forced leave of absence from both motorcycling and the Latin American world — my tour in Panama ended.

I sold my motorcycle and in 1975 the Army transferred me to Korea for two years and then to Washington, the one assignment I had worked to avoid for twenty-five years. I made a reluctant homecoming to a city that bore little resemblance to the tranquil setting of my boyhood years. Other than the opportunity to reunite with friends and relatives, the move had little appeal. It was mercifully short, however, and two years later I retired from the Army, putting into effect a long-held plan to move with my family to Florida.

3

The Obsession Rises

Far away is far away only if you don't go there.

O Povo
Fortaleza, Brazil

After more than half a lifetime of military service, responding automatically to commands and accepting regimentation without question, I no longer had to answer the bugler's call. I had trouble at first adjusting to my new freedom. I could not decide what drummer's beat to march to. Moving to Palm Bay, Florida, in early

1979 helped offset the retirement blues, and I gradually settled into a rather sedate, non-motorcycling life with few intrusions. But under the surface I had the disquieting feeling that something was missing, and I kept straining to hear another calling.

I continued to keep abreast of developments on the Pan American Highway. The United States had declared the entire interstate highway system to be part of the Pan Am. And the Alcan, which runs through Alaska and Canada, had been renamed the Alaska Highway and also included in the Pan Am system. The hemispheric highway had now tripled in length, and the main route ran almost as far north as it had originally extended south of the Rio Grande.

In Panama, however, the Pan Am was not faring as well. The Sierra Club successfully enjoined the Federal Highway Administration from funding further development of the highway in the Darien region. Fearing the Pan Am would escalate development at the expense of the area's Indians and the fragile rain forest environment, the club argued that the United States should not promote the uncontrolled growth the highway would inevitably stimulate.

In late 1979 I read a magazine article that stoked my wanderlust and revived my interest in motorcycling. I came across a four-year-old, tattered, well-read issue of *Cycle*, a motorcycling magazine. I don't even remember where I got the copy. But it carried a story titled "The Long Tour." Written by a Canadian adventurer named John Pitt, the article was a fascinating account, illustrated with magnificent photographs, of Pitt's motorcycle trip from Canada to Ushuaia, Argentina, on Tierra del Fuego at the tip of South America. What captivated me in reading the story over and over was not only the ride to Cape Horn and back, but that at the time of his journey Pitt was sixty-four years old!

Pitt's story affected me deeply. If Pitt could do it at his age, why couldn't I do it in my early fifties? Why shouldn't I revive that dream I had in Panama of motorcycling the Pan American Highway into the Southern Hemisphere?

I knew I was pondering a momentous decision. I would have to forsake my new second career in real estate. And I would have to temporarily abandon my other responsibilities to embark on the kind of extended trip that had so often disrupted my family life while in the Army.

For years in Panama my wife Nell had watched my growing interest in motorcycling. Not wanting to ride herself, she graciously tolerated my meanderings and fended off more than her share of prying questions, "What do you think about his riding off to God knows where?" And here I was thinking about taking off again.

When I told friends what I was considering, many saw the idea as a foolhardy, middle-age-crisis antic that would surely lead to catastrophe. In my mind, though, it would be a carefully planned, skillfully executed, meticulous exercise in travel. But this was lost on those who thought I had been touched with a bit of madness. I couldn't argue that point satisfactorily, but what I could do was *do it*. That would settle the issue. So I made the decision to ride to Cape Horn and back.

My first step was to buy another motorcycle. I found a near-duplicate of the BMW I had had in Panama. The new bike, a BMW 800-cc touring model, was fully equipped for the long distance journey I wanted to make. I dubbed the bike "Black Beauty" because of the gleaming hue and matching ebony accessories. I carefully broke it in as I retaught myself the skills of riding and then began working out the details of my own "long tour."

This trip would not be a repeat of my earlier runs to Panama. Times had changed in Central America, violently so. Parts of Guatemala were becoming battle-grounds. The insurgency in El Salvador had engulfed the country. And the Sandinista revolution in Nicaragua had created new obstacles for travel along the previously tranquil Pan American Highway.

While the road to Panama would expose me to new risks, I was also concerned about the onward journey to South America. The Darien Gap still remained impass-able — although I had heard of a jeep expedition crash-ing its way through to Panama from Colombia as part of a well-financed publicity venture. But I had no well-heeled sponsors to pay for an attempted passage through the jungle, so I would have to devise a way to bypass the gap when I arrived in Panama.

I also faced administrative obstacles as well, such as securing travel documents for the motorcycle. Colombia, Ecuador and Peru had very restrictive customs regula-tions which required special arrangements to import ve-hicles. I would have to secure a *Carnet de Passages en Douane,* an international bonding document that facili-tates vehicle travel through countries whose extremely high import taxes encourage illegal importation and sale of vehicles. So I put up a three-thousand-dollar bond for my *Carnet*. If I failed for any reason to bring the motorcycle out of any of the three countries, even if the bike was stolen, I would have to pay an exorbitant import duty or forfeit the bond.

One of my last tasks before setting out was to attach a new license plate to the bike, a personalized tag that read EE UU-1 — the Spanish version of USA-1. Remembering my Panama experiences with the Canal Zone M-1 tag, I hoped another distinctive plate would create the same kind of uncertain respect for me and the motorcycle.

I began my journey on an unusually cold Florida morning in late February 1980. Throughout my preparations I had been supremely confident and eager to get on with the venture. Yet barely thirty miles from home, when I stopped to re-rig my gear, volleys of apprehension blasted me.

"How in hell can you even think of a wild scheme like this, much less pull it off?" I asked myself.

This would not be the last moment of apprehension and hesitation, but I would not let the recurring surges of doubt force me to turn back.

I ran fast for Mexico and hurried on south through Central America. I bypassed violence-wracked El Salvador by traveling the back roads of northern Honduras. Nicaragua with its Cuban-advised bureaucracy, however, was a real concern in light of my intelligence background.

In addition to my overt intelligence activities in Panama, I had been involved in the Cuban exile movement in Miami in ways that probably earned me a spot on Castro's counterintelligence watch list. I thought the

Nicaraguans would not be a problem. The Sandinista revolution was still in its disorganized post-victory stage, and I counted on the government not functioning well enough to pose a hazard to me. But if some savvy Cuban security advisor ran a name check back through his computer system in Havana, or even on to the main frame in Moscow, I would be brought under suspicion. Fortunately, I passed through Nicaragua without difficulty.

I rode easily through Costa Rica and into Panama. I put up at the Road Knights Motorcycle Club at Albrook Air Force Station near Balboa. The club had been formed when I was stationed in Panama, and I still knew some of the older members, the civilians who maintained continuity throughout a constantly changing military membership. The club was a haven for bikers passing along the Pan Am, offering them lodging, companionship and repair facilities.

I caught up on the changes in Panama. The United States had signed the Panama Canal treaties eliminating the Canal Zone, and the Panamanian flag was now flying atop Ancon Hill. The U.S.-controlled Panama Canal Company had been renamed and reorganized and was now the Panama Canal Commission, staffed jointly by the United States and Panama. Many of my old Canal Zone friends and acquaintances had left the country after the treaties were ratified.

General Torrijos was basking in the glow of his international diplomatic triumph in getting the agreements written and signed. He continued to rely heavily on the head of his intelligence and security service, Lieutenant Colonel Noriega. Although still content to remain in the shadow of Torrijos, the wily Noriega lived up to his reputation as a master schemer and manipulator. Noriega was still nominally under the control of his U.S. Army counterparts, but he often showed irritating independence when it came to covert dealings with the Russians, Cubans and Sandinistas.

I asked about the Darien to confirm there was no way to get through the gap. Although the Bayano River bridge had been completed and the road extended well into the interior, over one hundred miles still separated the end of the road in Panama and its reappearance in Colombia. The rainy season had already started, and that meant the Darien would be impassable for the next nine months.

I found out that the publicity-seeking expedition that had come through the Darien from Colombia last year consisted of a caravan of five American Motors Corporation Jeeps. The vehicles were on a hemispheric trek from Ushuaia on Tierra del Fuego to Alaska. Expedition members drove five Jeeps north to Turbo, Colombia. From Turbo they shipped the vehicles by boat up the Atrato River and its tributaries to a point near the Panamanian border. Then, using air resupply and a small army of Indians equipped with power tools, the crews cut a path to winch their vehicles through the Darien to the end of the road near Cañazas. Regaining the highway, the AMC team drove the Jeep convoy along the remainder of the Pan Am to Alaska. The elaborate expedition garnered AMC much publicity and substantial promotional rewards to repay the tremendous expenses.

But that kind of adventuring was well beyond my

limited means. Without corporate backing of any kind, I had to find the cheapest way to get Black Beauty and myself around the Darien. My solution was to crate the bike and consign it to a Delta Lines freighter sailing from Balboa to Guayaquil, Ecuador. I followed by hitching a ride on a military flight from Panama to Bogotá and then transferring to buses to reach Guayaquil.

I picked up the bike from the shipping line and went on to duplicate Pitt's ride, reaching Tierra del Fuego and Ushuaia — the southern-most city in the world — with only minor tribulations. I made the return trip north via Brazil, where I expensively avoided the Darien again by flying myself and the bike back to Panama.

I spent several days at the Road Knights club refurbishing Black Beauty. The bike was no longer a pristine machine, but a well-scarred veteran of the Pan American Highway campaign.

When I set out for home I decided to take on El Salvador. I raced through the country, skirting around the Pan Am's blown bridges and seeing only brief glimpses of other war damage. But neither side troubled me. I simply moved too fast for the combatants to react to my headlong run through the war zones. I sped through Guatemala and crossed over into Mexico. Another five days of riding put me back in Florida, grateful to be home with my family.

Relieved of the pressures of travel, I could review the events of the past three months and five days. I had spent six thousand dollars, traveled twenty-six thousand miles through fifteen Latin American countries and suffered the administrative traumas of twenty-eight border crossings. But as I went over the trip in my mind,

I began to realize that the journey had produced effects that were not measurable in terms of time, cost and distance.

The trip had changed me. By riding to Cape Horn and back I had subjected myself to long periods of heavy introspection, the kind of thought only solitary travel can produce. Riding in isolation for thousands of miles, buffeted by the vagaries of weather, road and machine, I thought of the future and wondered just where this experience would fit into the life ahead of me. The trek had revived a restless spirit that made a return to orderly, conventional living seem impossible. Motorcycling had been a central part of my daily routine for the last three months, and I was determined to continue riding as long as I could swing a leg up and over the saddle.

The seed planted in my mind when I was stationed in Panama had indeed germinated into a run along the Pan Am through South America. The journey to Tierra del Fuego had been a resounding Personal Best, but except for me it hardly established a precedent. It was not the sort of Guinness Book feat that included a record-setting performance. All I had done was duplicate the deeds of other riders before me: John Pitt, more than a decade older than me, and Phil Funnell, another BMW rider who made the trip to Tierra del Fuego in much less time. I had also read in L.J.K. Setright's *Guinness Book of Motorcycling Facts and Feats* about a Nebraskan named Danny Liska who had logged ninety-five thousand miles along the Pan Am from Alaska to Argentina in the course of a circumnavigation of the world by north-south longitudinal routes. Now *that* was the kind of motorcycling that counted!

Reminders of the highway to the south kept coming to my attention. The U.S. Federal Highway Administration cut back funding for the Pan Am project and shut down field offices in Panama and Colombia. And the possibility of extinction loomed over the Organization of American States Darien Gap Highway Subcommittee — the dedicated *Darienistas*. I wondered how such events would affect the Pan Am and whether I would ever have the chance to ride south again.

I continued to dwell on the road. It seemed to be beckoning me to return, drawing me back for a more meaningful journey. As the Pan Am played on my mind, my obsession was quietly born. I realized what I had to do. I decided to go for a record — to become the first motorcyclist to travel the entire length of the main route of the Pan American Highway between Alaska and Argentina, including the proposed route through the Darien Gap. No other biker had done this, not even the world-circling Danny Liska.

My 1980 trip had been an invaluable lesson in cycling throughout Latin America, but I had made it in a conventional manner. I stayed on the main roads, sleeping in motels and aggressively working the old-boy network of Panama-era friends to help me along the way.

This trip would be different. Most of my friends were now gone, transferred to other duty stations or faded away to retirement back home. But above all, I had the Darien Gap to confront. I was now facing travel through rain forests, jungles and swamps to get through the Darien. I regretted not gaining more experience in the bush while in Southeast Asia and Panama. I should have attended the Jungle Operations Training Center or done more than just jump out of airplanes with the Green Berets. Somehow I would have to compensate for my lack of experience and skill at surviving in the boondocks. I figured planning would be the equalizer — the same kind of deliberate, detailed advance work that often substitutes for luck. I would use the old Army approach, the Seven Ps: Proper Prior Planning Prevents Piss-Poor Performance.

In 1983 I made a concrete commitment to the project. I set out to find a motorcycle that had Black Beauty's inherent reliability but fewer amenities and accessories that would add unwanted weight and bulk when making the Darien passage. After shopping around, I found that BMW had come out with the ideal machine. The Germans had developed an R80 G/S model — a replica of the bike they had used with great success in the grueling Paris-Dakar endurance run. Unlike any other motorcycle on the market at the time, it had a high, enduro-style front fender, spoke wheels, knobby tires for off-road traction and an upswept muffler to allow fording. It looked awkward and ungainly, but it had the same reliable two-cylinder engine as my earlier BMWs. And it promised to be the right machine for the mix of challenges I was facing.

The G/S was full of surprises. Riding away from the dealer's shop, I found the bike remarkably light and agile on the street, and it cruised exceedingly well on the open roads. It also could survive off the road. Although much heavier than other enduro motorcycles, the simple, rugged 800-cc engine could power the bike confidently through the worst patches of sand and gravel.

I now regretted not having had the G/S for my 1980

South American trip. I was convinced that this was the only machine that had the versatility to ride comfortably along the Interstates, to navigate the gravel roads of the Alaska Highway and to carry me — or vice versa as it would often turn out — through the Darien jungles.

My plan called for dividing the run into four phases. Phase One would take me from Florida to Laredo, Texas, where I would pick up the main route of the Pan American Highway, and then on to Panama. There I would prepare for Phase Two, getting through the Darien Gap and on to Bogotá, Colombia. By attacking the Darien at the outset when both the bike and I were fresh, I would increase my chances of success.

In Phase Three I intended to head south from Bogotá, riding the Pan Am through Ecuador, Peru, and into Chile. Near Santiago, Chile, the Pan Am turns east, and I would ride the highway across Argentina to reach Buenos Aires. Then I would head back north, touching the capitals of Uruguay, Brazil and Venezuela. This time the bike and I would either fly or take a ship to Panama to get around the Darien Gap and continue north to Laredo. Phase Four, Texas to Alaska, would be a fairly easy run through the lower United States, Canada and on to Fairbanks, Alaska.

Although excitement and enthusiasm gnawed at me to get on with the adventure, I disciplined myself to stick with the Seven Ps. I now had to map out a campaign to conquer the gap, because the success or failure of my expedition hinged on beating this formidable obstacle. To set out now, ad-libbing the Darien passage, would unnecessarily risk disaster.

I reluctantly decided to go back to Panama to further

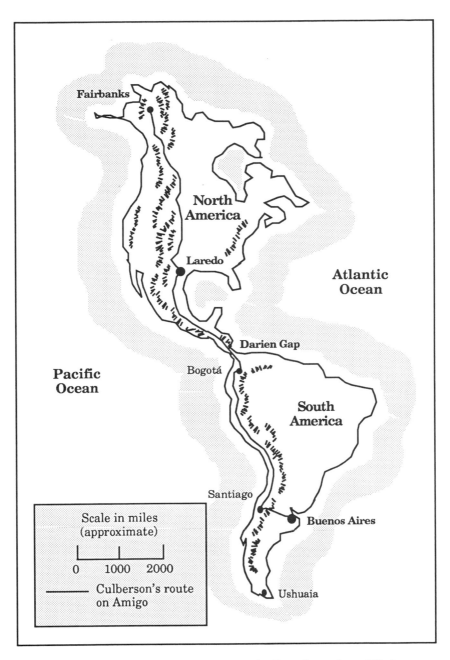

**Ed Culberson's route along the main Pan American Highway
Fairbanks, Alaska — Buenos Aires, Argentina**

investigate the Darien before actually launching the full-scale assault. I would make a reconnaissance trip to find out just what it would take to get through the gap. With the Darien's dry season extending at best from late December to late March, the reconnaissance trip meant I would have to postpone the actual run for another year. But better the delay than to blunder into an area that had been the site of disaster and death for many unsuspecting adventurers.

4

Folly and Madness

What you are proposing to do, Señor,
is a cross between folly and madness.

Consul Martinez
Yaviza, Panama, 1984

Pressured by time and hobbled by a lack of money, I garaged the G/S and flew from Miami to Panama in February, 1984. I landed at the new Omar Torrijos International Airport, named for the popular leader who had died in a 1981 plane crash. I set up again at the Road Knights Motorcycle Club, reuniting with the long-term civilian members I knew from before. They introduced me to a new crew of military riders who had rotated in during the last four years.

I checked the club logbook which had added quite a few pages since I had last signed in. I saw a few cryptic references to the Darien, but no indication that any cyclists had succeeded in passing through the gap. According to the accommodating club custodian, Khim Rojas, there had been riders who had full intentions of biking onward to South America through the Darien. Apparently, however, none had been able to complete a passage through the gap.

My ten days in Panama turned into a whirlwind of reconnaissance and research, much of it frustrating. The damned Darien almost beat me at the outset. The Pan Am had now been extended as an unpaved road into the Darien region to the town of Yaviza, shrinking the gap to about eighty miles. I had arranged to borrow a bike and ride the 180 miles from Panama City to the end of the road. But Rojas warned me that the newest section of the Pan Am in the Darien region had reportedly been closed to traffic.

I confirmed the closing with a Panamanian official. "Sí, señor, es imposible. La ruta está bloqueada," he said. The dry season had not yet ended, but an early rainstorm had washed out part of the road near Yaviza.

So now I had to resort to Plan Two. Early the next morning I took a cab to Paitilla Airport, the commuter airfield adjacent to Panama City. There I caught the early-morning flight out to the Darien in a lumbering, two-engine Britten-Norman Islander, overloaded with both passengers and cargo.

The aircraft skirted the mangrove swamps guarding the coast and entered the Gulf of San Miguel where the pilot made a flying-school landing on a rough gravelled strip next to the fishing village of La Palma. We traded some passengers and cargo and then took off following the Tuira River toward El Real de Santa Maria, the unofficial capital of the Darien region and a centuries-old Spanish exploration base.

As the plane made its approach to a concrete runway of World War II vintage, I peered through the window to check the weather inland toward Yaviza. Sure enough, the almost perpetual cloud cover was hanging in there. If that overcast kept the pilot from locating and setting down on Yaviza's dirt strip, he would turn back to Panama City. So I decided to deplane at El Real.

I hitched a ride from the airfield into town on a rusted, cantankerous three-quarter ton truck. The driver told me it was surplus property left over from when the U. S. Army Air Corps had built the airstrip for anti-submarine patrols during the Big War. It was the only motorized land vehicle around — I didn't even see a dirt bike.

But there were outboard motors, one of which was hanging on a sawhorse in front of the town's single hotel. The only way in or out of El Real is by air or river, and the river now had to be my route to Yaviza. A grease-stained man was working on the ancient outboard. I talked with him, and he said he had a boat to match the motor and would be willing to take me up-river as soon as he finished the tune-up.

I used the wait to enjoy a badly needed breakfast of spicy sausages, eggs, bread and coffee at the hotel. After a quick tour of the town, I returned to find the man had finished working on the engine and had hauled it to the nearby riverbank. There he had attached it to the stern of a battered piragua — a dugout canoe.

We discussed the fare.

"¿Cuanto cuesta?" I asked.

"No mucho," the swarthy Panamanian replied. *"Solamente el precio de la gasolina."*

It sounded too good that I would only have to pay the fuel cost for the outboard motor. And it was. Not only did I have to buy enough gas for the trip to Yaviza, but also for the return trip, which I learned was the custom when hiring boats in the Darien. Worse yet, when we stopped at a nearby primitive riverine gas depot, the fuel cost four dollars a gallon!

We sputtered upriver, threading our way through muddy, rain-swollen channels clotted with jungle debris. I quickly learned that in a piragua my instinctive cycling habit of adding body English and leaning into curves wasn't helpful. That tactic only increased the alarming intake of water over the canoe's alarmingly low freeboard.

When we reached Yaviza disappointment clouded my relief. The settlement was nothing more than a collection of weathered board shacks gathered high on the banks of the Chucunaque River. Yaviza had far fewer amenities and even less charm than El Real. Other than its location near the junction of the Chucunaque and Chico rivers, it seemed an illogical place for the Northern Hemisphere terminus of the Pan American Highway.

I wandered along the town's two sets of rough concrete-and-dirt streets which were flanked by unpainted houses, several small stores and dubious eating places. I saw no vehicles of any sort, and I was puzzled by the apparent lack of impact the new road had had on the town since the inauguration of the link to Panama City the year before.

Obviously logistics would be a problem in staging for the Darien. The rude set of cribs that posed as a hotel was not inviting as a base camp. And the town did not even have a reliable supply of gasoline. So far, Yaviza did not have enough motor vehicle traffic to warrant adding gasoline stocks to the predominant gas-oil pre-mix used in the outboard motors of the watercraft.

If this was Yaviza, I wondered what it would be like beyond here on the route to Colombia. Would it actually be possible to push on and make it to the border? And from there could I get the bike through the swamps and across the Atrato River to the beginning of the road in South America?

I nosed around Yaviza, talking to people and trying to find out the routes taken by earlier expeditions. Few people remembered any details about Webb and Merrill, the two Panama Canal employees who had wandered through on their small dual-drive Rokon motorcycles. But most Yavizans recalled the massive onslaught of the 1979 American Motors Jeep expedition, which had employed a well-paid horde of local guides, porters and trail cutters. I also heard vague stories of a jeep crew headed by a tall, thin gringo named Loren Upton. He had struggled out to Yaviza and beyond several times and was once forced to turn back when a crew member died mysteriously.

Backpackers and even an occasional bicyclist had

trekked through Yaviza from both directions. Several venturesome motorcyclists from Panama had made recent visits to Yaviza, but none had crossed the Chucunaque River intending to cut their way through to the border and on to Colombia. I was reassured that nobody had seen or heard of any motorcycles other than the Rokons setting out for or arriving from Colombia. The proposed route of the Pan Am through the Darien and on to the southern terminus in Colombia was still unconquered by a motorcyclist.

One Yaviza native, Sergeant Morales of the Panama Defense Forces — the new name for the Guardia Nacional — told me of another danger I needed to be concerned about.

"Sí, mi amigo, es posible viajar a la frontera Colombiana, pero los drogistas son muy peligrosos."

Yes, I might be able to reach the Colombian border, but the biggest danger would be from drug smugglers. Sergeant Morales said they would kill to avoid any interference in their trade. An easy-going career soldier, the sergeant smiled at me paternally and said, "there are already people here who have assumed you are an agent of the U.S. Drug Enforcement Administration."

I felt naked at this second-hand accusation. I hoped that when I came back with my motorcycle, the bike would deflect any suspicions about the purpose of my visit to Yaviza and my journey into the Darien.

I also talked with the local representative of the Colombian government. Señor Martinez had his office in a primitive, thatch-roofed "consulate." I couldn't help but wonder what gross career error he had made to warrant being banished to this godforsaken outpost. An excitable and officious man, Señor Martinez was concerned about my goal. He anxiously cautioned me against a cross-border passage through the Darien. It had been done by hikers, bicyclists and by expeditions equipped with rugged four-wheel drive vehicles he said, but to attempt crossing the Darien alone with a motorcycle was *una locura* — a cross between folly and madness.

After hours of asking questions, I began the task of finding a way back to Panama City. With the road still blocked I had to find another route or wait until the next "maybe" flight out of Yaviza's muddy airstrip.

But good fortune came along in the form of a sympathetic local official who offered me a spot on his fourteen-foot boat going up the Chucunaque. The craft would head for a point close to the open section of the Pan American Highway. The official said one of the six passengers had a truck there and would take me back to Canglón, where I could board a bus to return to Panama City. I jumped at the chance to scout the road back. This would make up in part for not being able to ride the bike out to Yaviza.

As the small boat made its way upriver, I rode more comfortably and felt much safer than on the morning's piragua excursion to Yaviza. But the bliss lasted only until we nosed into the steep, slippery riverbank and the boatman signalled me to disembark. I lost my footing jumping from the prow and resorted to crawling up the bank on all fours, to the amusement of the other passengers.

That seemed to set the mood for the five-mile trek that followed, a march that was a preview of what I could expect in the eastern Darien. We slogged through thick underbrush following a faint trail that several men had to enlarge with skilled machete strokes. Nevertheless, they set a fast pace and I quickly became drenched with sweat.

Up ahead I could hear some of the Panamanians talking loudly, and one man repeatedly made loud grunting noises and guttural shouts as he cut away the dangling vines and low branches. I asked the man ahead of me about the curious sounds.

"He's signalling to the snakes that we are on the trail, so they can get out of our way."

I seriously considered adding my gringo voice to the native chorus.

Through occasional breaks in the heavy undergrowth I caught glimpses of small plots of cultivated land and a thatched hut or two. Finally we broke into a clearing. Now I could see the new road — a muddy red track showing the latticed scars of earthmover cleats. And I could hear the roar of the machines in the distance.

The road was dreadful. Thick, gooey mud pulled at my boots, quickly making each step a struggling aerobic exercise. The exertion compounded my now-maddening thirst. Before long, I felt near to exhaustion. And I glumly remembered that this was the same area through which Lieutenant Strain and his disoriented party had wandered about so many years ago.

We reached our destination, a road construction camp, and my companions scrounged cups of tepid water which I greedily shared. Heat, humidity, thirst and mud had all combined to sap my strength. They were adversaries I would have to face again, and I knew I would have to devise strong defenses against them.

In addition to the heavy road-building equipment, the camp held a collection of vehicles that included a pickup truck and a motorcycle. During our respite I took a closer look at the bike — a small Honda owned by one of our party, Florencio Gonzalez. He was a mechanic and a transplanted western Panamanian. Florencio was proud to own the only motorcycle east of the Bayano River. And despite the rough environment, he maintained the cycle well. It was a dirt bike, an ideal machine for the area, and I congratulated him on both his choice of wheels and the bike's condition. He was modest, but forthright when I asked him if he would risk taking the bike through the gap to Colombia.

"Yes," he replied quickly, "but only in the company of reliable friends and with the right supplies and equipment. And with Indians to cut the trail."

I liked his response. Florencio was a latter-day pioneer. Having severed ties with his family in the west, he had emigrated to the newly opened Darien region via the Pan American Highway. He would be the kind of man I would want with me in the wilderness beyond the Chucunaque River.

Florencio mounted the Honda and almost effortlessly kick-started the pliant engine and wheeled down the muddy, rutted road. The pickup truck owner, Javier Tapia, motioned me aboard. We followed the motorcycle, wallowing through the slop until the road stabilized into crimson laterite which then yielded to gravel as we approached Canglón, a newly created colony astride the road.

It was far too late to catch a *chiva*, one of the small buses that ran back to Panama City, so Javier invited

me to stay with him at his half-finished house. I spent a
restless night on the bare wooden floor, and I found out
how persistent the Darien mosquitoes could be. I wished
my insect repellant was more potent and worried about
the malaria potential of the buzzing, swarming insects.

In the morning Javier offered to take me to Panama
City in the truck, and I savored the comfort of the cab
which allowed me to gauge the 160 miles of road as we
headed westward. The road initially ran through thick
stands of bamboo, palms and massive ceiba trees, and as
we piled up the miles and headed out of the Darien
region, the clouds dissipated and the climate grew increasingly drier.

At Cañazas, near the Choco Indian settlement along
the Ipetí River, we had to stop for a PDF police identity
check and malaria test. I looked at my map and saw we
were now well beyond the point on the highway where
in 1513 Balboa and his band of explorers had struggled
across the isthmus to stand "silent upon a peak in Darien" in awe of the sight of the Pacific Ocean.

Back at Balboa, I returned to the Road Knights clubhouse to continue my research. I spent days tracking
down leads and thumbing through old news reports at
the Panama Canal Commission library and talking to
commission authorities and military officials.

I interviewed veterans of the Isthmian Four-Wheeler
Club at their facility beside the Panama Canal Miraflores Locks. The club hosts visiting automotive travelers, and its members periodically venture out into the
jungle regions. Club members said it had been over five

years since anyone had tried to penetrate the gap, despite its being squeezed down to about eighty miles.

I found the reduction of the gap most promising. It was far narrower now than when earlier expeditions, including Webb and Merrill on their Rokons, had struggled so hard just to reach Yaviza. I felt the project was now doable and would take far less resources and time than past expeditions had required.

I compiled a list of Darien Gap vehicular expeditions and began plotting their routes. I started with the OAS-National Geographic exploration, which the late Jose March had credited with destroying the Myth of the Darien, and included all the unsuccessful attempts I was able to uncover. Surprisingly, I found little information on the AMC Jeep expedition and even less on the convoy of Chevrolet Corvairs.

I met another major frustration when I discovered the surprising lack of available maps of the Darien. I visited the *Instituto Geográfico Nacional* "Tommy Guardia" — the Panamanian Geographic Institute, named in memory of Tomas Guardia, Junior, one of the most fanatic *Darienistas*. The staff could offer only outdated maps and sketchy drawings that gave little of the detail needed by expeditioners.

The institute's maps were also woefully inaccurate, as I would find out later. The torrential rains of the Darien's rainy season frequently wash away surface features, alter the course of streams and rivers and force relocation of entire villages. Even the U. S. military topographic maps depicted ground features of admittedly dubious reliability or showed numerous areas labeled "relief data irreconcilable."

By now I had run out of time and money and would have to return to Florida. Regretfully, I was leaving behind many unanswered questions and was still disappointed at not being able to explore further into the gap. But I had become acutely aware of just how formidable a challenge the Darien's tropical wilderness would be.

Just before leaving, I read a quotation on a bronze tablet in the rotunda of the Panama Canal Commission building. Inscribed on it were the words of Theodore Roosevelt, the first U.S. president to travel abroad while in office, who had come to Panama in 1906 to inspect the canal-building project.

It is not the critic who counts; not the man who points out how the strong man stumbled, or where the doer of deeds could have done them better. The credit belongs to the man who is actually in the arena, whose face is marred by dust and sweat and blood, who strives valiantly, who errs and comes short again and again; who knows the great enthusiasms, the great devotions, and spends himself in a worthy cause, who, at the best, knows in the end the triumph of great achievement; and who, at the worst, if he fails, at least fails while daring greatly, so that his place shall never be with those cold and timid souls who know neither victory nor defeat.

These were lofty words, spoken in an era more appropriate to the towering ambitions of someone like Balboa or even Loren Upton, the man I had heard about in Yaviza who had repeatedly tried almost single-handedly to get a vehicle through the Darien.

But I was moved by Teddy's words. They bolstered my resolve to return to Panama, to again head eastward beyond the Chagres and Bayano rivers and to go back into the Darien to take up my own version of a "worthy cause."

5

The Precarious Partnership

Lead, and I follow.

Tennyson
Idylls of the King

Back home in Florida, I distilled the data from my Yaviza trip into a coherent picture. I still worried over the immensity of the project, but I consoled myself that *el Tapón* had been narrowed to only about eighty miles. Despite my concerns, I was more determined than ever to continue the quest. The trip had stoked my obsession to get through the gap and ride the entire main Pan American Highway. I committed myself to the next dry season — January through March 1985.

Señor Martinez, the Colombian consul in Yaviza, was probably right. To try to get through the gap alone would be foolhardy. But I thought the right combination of motorcycles, equipment and determined riders could breach The Stopper. So I began casting about for help from sponsors, potential partners — anyone who hungered for a bit of adventure and who would be willing to share not only the rewards but the burdens as well.

I put the concept on paper, describing the Yaviza reconnaissance trip, and invited other adventurers to join me on a concerted assault on the gap. A motorcycle magazine, *Rider,* printed two of my articles along with introductory remarks by the publisher, Denis Rouse. He restated the magazine's concept of "adventure touring," and said the Darien project "...may be the most adventurous of all."

The articles generated immediate responses. I began receiving letters and calls from would-be expeditioners from all over the country. Some wanted to participate, others wanted more information, a few simply offered encouragement. John Pitt, the Canadian biker whose article had spurred me on in 1980, wrote apologetically of his desire to participate in the journey but said he would be unable to ride with me.

Unfortunately, the interest proved mostly unproductive. Unlike John, most respondents didn't really understand the nature or the magnitude of the task. They could not work with the many constraints such as the timing of the expedition which was dictated solely by the

Darien's short dry season. Or they could not afford to secure their *Carnet de Passages en Douane,* needed for the onward travel in South America.

But the *Rider* magazine stories did eventually deliver a valuable lead. Quite by chance I encountered a motorcycling friend who had read the articles, and he referred me to an American living in Bogotá, Colombia. I had heard of this American before — he was Danny Liska, the Guinness book record holder who had toured the Pan Am while circumnavigating the world on a motorcycle. He gave me Liska's address and said Liska was working on a book about the Darien region. Liska would be an excellent source of background information, and I immediately wrote him for advice on my Darien idea.

My friend's referring me to Liska and my letter to him had a timing that seemed to go beyond sheer coincidence. Upon receiving my letter, Liska telephoned to say he was due to arrive in Florida in a week! He would be visiting the United States with his Colombian wife and a group of other Colombians. They would be in Orlando, only sixty miles from Palm Bay, and we agreed to meet and discuss the project.

We met at a restaurant near Disney World. My first impression of Liska was that he still fit the image BMW had cast him in for their advertisements almost a generation ago. Tall and almost hulking in girth, his dark countenance could have been menacing if it were not for his soft-spoken, courtly manner. The bear-like man had been born in Nebraska in 1929 of Czechoslovakian immigrant parents. Raised in rugged country, he became a natural wanderer and adventurer who savors life with a gusto seldom enjoyed by other men.

Liska earned his Guinness book recognition starting in 1958 when he rode his BMW motorcycle to the Arctic Circle in Alaska. Then he rode south toward Tierra del Fuego. He reached Panama during the rainy season and could not get through the Darien Gap with the motorcycle. Instead he made the passage on foot, surviving a near-drowning in a rain-swollen river and encounters with antagonistic Cuna Indians.

Resuming his motorcycle travel in Colombia, he rode on to the tip of South America. On his return he paused in Argentina where he became involved in the filming of the movie *Taras Bulba*. Reverting to his youthful affinity for horses, Liska shaved his head and doubled for Yul Brynner, the film's star, in the more dangerous horseback battle scenes.

Later he went to Germany where he picked up a new BMW motorcycle to complete the European and African portion of his circumnavigation by riding between Norway's North Cape and Cape Town, South Africa. He returned to South America and was passing through Colombia when he met and was immediately captivated by his present wife, Regina XI — a charismatic figure who matches Liska's engaging personality.

Regina was with Danny when I met him at the restaurant, and I was struck by her refined beauty and vivacious Latin manner. She is a self-proclaimed psychic who projects an aura that seems to justify her title as Regina XI. Danny said the eleven signifies her rank in the number of people who have been endowed with powers of the occult. She also is the leader of a religious and political group that is near-fanatical in her support.

Regina remained with the other Colombians as

Danny and I slipped away to discuss the Darien project. He was forthright with his advice.

"Ed, don't try it by yourself. I tried it years ago, and even without my motorcycle I barely made it out alive."

I told Danny about my background — the four years in Panama, the 1980 ride to Cape Horn and the reconnaissance trip to Yaviza. He was impressed, but not enough to offset his concern over the implications of what I was proposing to do.

Since fighting his way through the gap on foot in 1961, he had become a serious student of the area. He kept up with events and developments in the region while maintaining a cautious respect for the Darien which, following his harrowing experience, bordered on trepidation. I didn't immediately realize it, but his conversation was subtly trying to expose me to the idea of the Curse of the Darien.

I had difficulty at first handling Danny's obvious reluctance to cheer me on. I smugly believed that his expertise was dated — twenty-three years behind the times — and not in keeping with what I had found out about the Darien on my recent reconnaissance trip.

Unfortunately, my Orlando meeting with the Liskas was too short to develop a meaningful rapport, but it did set the stage for later contacts. And the next one came quickly, just shortly after Danny returned to Bogotá. He telephoned to tell me that a jeep expedition was fitting out in Panama City for an attempt at shooting the Darien Gap!

Liska told me how to contact the expedition's leader, an American named Loren Lee Upton — the man I had heard about when I was in Yaviza. Upton had made several attempts at the Darien, and Liska said he once succeeded in getting a jeep through to the Colombian side of the gap before having to abandon it. Liska's news electrified me, and I thought now was my chance to join up with a jungle expert, a man who obviously could confront and overcome the very obstacles I was worrying about.

I spent several days trying to reach Upton directly by telephone in Panama. A woman named Pat Mercier in the former Canal Zone served as an intermediary. A member of Upton's expedition, she would try to arrange a time when Upton could get to a telephone to take my call. Once we connected, we sparred cautiously from the outset, each trying to assess the other. Except for our mutual acquaintance with Danny Liska and our intense interest in a Darien passage, we seemed to have little to share. I pressed Upton for an invitation to join his party, but I could not get a firm commitment. "Come on down and let's talk it over face to face," he said. "Then we'll see how it looks."

Eager to grab onto the shirttail of an experienced Darien expeditioner, I failed to detect Upton's reserve at a stranger wanting to join his team. I should have realized he had good reason to be noncommittal. Life in the jungle would make short work of casual friendships. No expedition needed less than totally dedicated members, and to Upton, I was an unknown.

Timing was also critical. It was now January 1985, and Upton warned me he was planning to leave for the Darien as soon as possible. The dry season was at hand and he would move quickly once his jeep had been refurbished from its trip south from California.

I promised him I would be on the road as soon as I could. But I had much to do and a short time in which to do it. Once again I went about the infuriating task of securing another international vehicle travel document from the automobile association. This time I had to post a five-thousand-dollar bond for the *Carnet* and then wait a frustrating two weeks until it was issued.

I also had to service the motorcycle and shop for the special equipment I would need for the jungle. One comforting item I obtained was a special Florida license plate for the G/S: AMIGO. With anti-American feelings increasing in the Central American countries I would have to pass through on my return to Panama, I hoped the tag would deflect attention from me and focus it on the motorcycle.

I joyfully attached the gleaming green and white plate to the motorcycle, despite having committed a Spanish language grammatical error. The bike could not possibly be named Amigo. Motorcycles in the Latin world are considered feminine — *motocicletas* — therefore my new machine more properly should have been named Amiga.

No matter. I ignored the gaffe, and whenever a perceptive Latin commented on the misnomer, I reminded him or her that the name referred to the rider and not the bike. After all, I considered myself to be the amigo — a friend of the world. That always seemed to resolve the question.

But my preparations continued to drag on. And when completed, they added up to too much time lost to ride to Panama. Fearful of missing Upton, I rode from Palm Bay to Miami on February seventh and had the bike crated and flown to Panama. I followed on a passenger flight and rented a car at the airport to drive to the Road Knights clubhouse.

The next day I left the car at the Road Knights and walked less than a block to look up Pat Mercier. I found her at the Girl Scouts office, where she managed scouting activities in the Panama Canal area.

A pleasant, good-natured woman in her mid-thirties, Pat radiated enthusiasm for Upton's Darien expedition. She had become fascinated with Upton's plan to ride through the gap to Colombia and had accepted his invitation to join him. She had the credentials. She and her husband — a Panama Canal Commission employee — had much experience in four-wheel expeditions into the jungles of Panama. She had arranged for a month's leave of absence from her job and planned to leave her young daughter in her husband's care.

I asked Pat where I could contact Upton.

"Loren and his nephew are out at the Miraflores Locks," she replied. "They are staying at the Isthmian Four-Wheeler clubhouse. They're waiting to see you."

I drove the rental car up the Gaillard Highway alongside the canal, eager to meet the man who had accrued a reputation as a fanatic in his crusade to conquer the gap.

I knew immediately which of the two men sitting on a bench beside the clubhouse workshop was Loren Lee Upton. He was middle-aged with a craggy face and unkempt moustache. He had on a well-worn brown Smoky the Bear campaign hat and wore tattered, grease-stained coveralls. Upton and his younger companion eyed me warily as I left the rental car to walk toward them, picking my way among piles of rusted automotive parts.

"I'm looking for Loren Upton," I said redundantly.

"You've found him," he said, slowly rising to his six-foot, four-inch height. He extended a huge, calloused hand that had been braiding wire rope into eyelets for towing cables.

So this is Loren Upton, I thought. The man who had tried four times to drive a jeep through the Darien Gap. The man who Danny Liska and others said was born a hundred years too late, because he wanted to be an explorer and expeditioner of the same caliber as the brave men of centuries past.

He introduced me to his nephew, Lawrence Upton, a clean-cut, twenty-three-year-old man from Spokane, Washington. Lawrence had taken a leave from his job as a lumberman to join Upton's expedition.

"Where's the motorcycle?" Upton asked. I explained I was going to pick up Amigo the next day at the airport freight depot after getting the customs-clearance documents.

"Well, you'd better hurry, because we're moving out as soon as the jeep is ready to go. All we have to do is make a test run to check it out, and it's off to Yaviza for us."

I was taken aback that Upton seemed to have already included me in his expedition. Perhaps, I thought, my having flown down from Miami with the motorcycle indicated to him that I was indeed sincere and totally committed to the Darien adventure.

Elated at the ready acceptance and promise of an early start toward the jungle, I returned to the Road

Knights club to set up my own base. I declined Upton's offer to stay with him and Lawrence at the Four Wheeler clubhouse. The Road Knights offered a much cleaner, militarily neater setting, far more comfortable and familiar to me and closer to the facilities I would need to prepare Amigo and myself for the Darien.

The next day everything went smoothly, and I easily got Amigo uncrated and released from customs. I gleefully rode the bike back from the airport along the Pan American Highway to Balboa, knowing I would soon be heading in the other direction, abandoning the comforts of the canal area and venturing into the Darien.

At the Road Knights I stripped the bike down to save every ounce of weight possible. I took off the windshield, turn signals, mirrors and any other equipment I thought not essential to running in the jungle. I disconnected the headlight and brake light and loosened the clutch and brake levers so they would not break off during any falls on the trails.

I laid out all my personal gear and carefully evaluated each item as to whether it was an absolute necessity. I consigned the nonessentials to a storage locker at the clubhouse. What little I could take had to fit into my tank bag, a zippered nylon bag strapped atop the gas tank, or into a backpack to be carried in Upton's jeep. My only bulky item was a canvas jungle hammock — a combined sleeping pad and canopy tied together with mosquito netting — that could be strung up between trees to keep me off the ground.

I found the preparations exciting. They fueled my increasing anticipation for the assault on the gap in company with a man who had been there before. I concluded that Upton could take measure of the job at hand as few others could.

But on my next visit to the Four Wheeler clubhouse I immediately got an uneasy feeling that my excitement might be premature. Upton was much more reserved than at our first meeting. He was not unfriendly, but it was apparent he had something to say.

"Ed," he said sternly, looking at me intently with his piercing blue eyes, "I can get you through to Bogotá, but what can you do for me?"

I was confounded. Based on our first conversation I thought he had accepted me as a member of his crew unconditionally without any specific requirement on my part.

"You can't make it on your own," he said. "I'm going to get you through because I know how. I've driven a jeep through the gap twice before, which is more than anyone else has ever done. You need me, but I don't need you. So what can you do to pay your way?"

He had caught me off guard, and I had trouble responding with a meaningful answer. I stumbled and finally offered my talents as a photographer and Spanish linguist, services which I was sure he needed badly.

Upton accepted my reply without comment and then pressed me for more answers.

"Why are you trying to get through the gap?"

He stared at me as I tried to explain what motivated me to want to ride the entire Pan Am by motorcycle.

"I'm doing it for the same reason you're trying to drive your jeep all the way around the world," I said.

I had concluded that Upton was driven by a far more burning obsession than mine. He wanted to set a record by driving a vehicle from Alaska to Cape Horn and then from South Africa to the North Cape of Norway. By driving through the Darien Gap instead of flying or boating around it as others had done, Upton would perform a feat greatly exceeding that of any previous Western Hemisphere expeditioner.

If he succeeded, he would be the only adventurer to have driven a vehicle around the world by a longitudinal route completely by land, except for the necessary ocean passages. He would earn a place in the record books for having accomplished an extremely difficult feat of travel and "romantic high adventure," as he so frequently termed his expeditions. He would rank alongside his heroes, the legendary explorers whose exploits he could readily recite.

But Upton seemed almost suspicious of my motives. I gave him copies of my magazine stories, and he quizzed me on just what I intended to do and write about after completing my Pan American Highway project. He was practically cross-examining me. The situation came close to deteriorating into a contest of wills when he listed his requirements for me to accompany him on the expedition.

"I want you to sign an agreement to pay half the costs of the expedition, starting the day we head into the Darien," he said firmly. "I'm in the expedition business and that's the fee for my services. And anything you write has to be approved by me. I will review all your journals each day to see that you are reporting the facts correctly. And I expect to get copies of all your photos and to share equally in any royalties or other payments you receive as a result of being with me."

I was astounded. I began to protest, but he cut me off. He said that people, including Danny Liska — whom he had assumed was a friend — had written unflattering articles about him. He specifically cited Danny's reporting on the mysterious death of his photographer in an earlier Darien Gap expedition. I asked Upton for time to consider his proposals, and I left deeply disturbed but promising to return the next day.

I understood Upton's bitterness over the events that followed the death of his photographer. The incident had put a traumatic end to his attempt to get through the gap in 1976. His vehicle, a converted telephone repair truck, had broken down near Yaviza, and Upton had left the photographer to guard the truck and their belongings while he returned to Panama City for parts. The photographer was found shot to death, and upon Upton's return the Guardia Nacional attempted to implicate him in the crime. After weeks of investigation, the Guardia finally released Upton for lack of evidence and he left Panama.

Even though I understood Upton's reasoning, I did not feel any better about his conditions for my joining the expedition. Upton, I reflected, had correctly assessed my position and was using my total dependence on his Darien experience to establish his supremacy. That was not a problem. I could accept his leadership without question or hesitation. I considered it nothing more than being assigned to a military unit headed by an eccentric or tyrannical commander, and I had had my share in the Army.

Upton's demand that I bear half the costs was unfair in terms of numbers. I knew I would need fewer supplies than Upton, Pat Mercier, Lawrence and the Jeep. But since he had established it as his fee, I could grudgingly agree to it. And besides, the added costs would end when we reached Bogotá — within a month according to the schedule Upton had set.

But Upton's requirement that he review my writing and share in any proceeds was simply unacceptable. As a writer, I could not let Upton censor my work. But there appeared to be more than censorship involved here. His wanting to examine my writing indicated he was insecure — he seemed afraid that I would somehow adversely expose him.

I spent a restless night silently debating an approach to Upton's requirements. And I mentally prepared a bargaining position that I thought would bridge the chasm that had suddenly opened between us.

The next day I returned to Miraflores and invited Upton to reopen negotiations. He was wary and said little as I offered my concessions. Yes, I would pay a half share of the costs and give him a one-thousand-dollar cash advance, promising to cover my share of any expenses that might go beyond that. I also restated my qualifications as an interpreter and photographer. And I offered to share copies of my writings and photography with him, but not on condition of prior approval or splitting whatever payments they might bring.

Upton listened noncommittally. Then he leaned back and stared at me. I could tell he was not satisfied.

"All that's fine, Ed, but what else can you do to make it work?"

Now, I thought, it's time for the heavy artillery. When the Guardia Nacional had interrogated Upton on the death of his photographer, the head of the security service had been Lieutenant Colonel Noriega. Now, General Noriega was not only the commandant of the Panama Defense Forces, the former Guardia Nacional, but also the dictator of the country. Surely, Noriega would have been kept informed of Upton's return to Panama. Given his past experience, this might be part of Upton's insecurity. I was sure Upton would have a deep dread of Noriega and the Panama Defense Forces.

"Loren, you know that I was stationed here while I was in the Army. During that time General Noriega gave me a letter permitting me to travel in restricted areas along the Costa Rican border. What if I could get him to give me another letter allowing me — or us — to pass through the Darien?"

That did it. Upton got excited as I showed him the 1975 letter signed by Noriega on the Guardia Nacional's G-2 letterhead, and he eagerly accepted the idea.

I left and set about making my offer good. Danny Liska and his wife were in Panama City, and I had previously arranged to meet them at their downtown hotel. They were here so Regina XI could perform her psychic services — and her principal client was General Noriega!

I told the Liskas of my problems and negotiations with Upton. "Danny," I pleaded, "I need you and Regina XI to help me get to Noriega. I could try through my old military contacts, but I don't think they would work anymore, especially for a completely unofficial deal like this."

"OK, Ed," he said, "let's take a look at that letter and see how we can work this out."

He carefully read the letter and agreed that a new version might be the right approach.

"I don't think Noriega will grant you an audience. There's nothing in this for him, so you'll probably be turned down if you ask to see him," Danny said.

Regina suggested, "Why not let me work it out through my dear friend Gaby Maher? If anyone can get Manuel's attention, it will be her."

The name struck a responsive chord with me. I had heard of Gaby and recalled that she was an influential woman who moved easily in official circles. Danny and I agreed that Regina's plan appeared to be the ideal solution. I gave the safe-passage letter to Danny and Regina, along with updated information showing my retired rank, the new motorcycle — Amigo — and the Darien region and Colombia as the area of travel.

Regina's plan worked. Within a day the Liskas notified me that Gaby had coaxed the General into issuing an updated version of the letter. They told me to pick it up at Gaby's palatial home in an affluent Panama City suburb. I never got to meet Gaby, however. Her young son hailed me on the street in front of the home and handed me the letter.

On the way back to Miraflores I converted one thousand dollars in travelers checks to U. S. dollars, which are used by Panama as its medium of exchange. I presented the bulky packet of small-denomination bills and the Noriega letter to Upton, completing my part of the agreement we had worked out.

He accepted them almost without comment. He was preoccupied with his jeep, which had developed problems. Since our first meeting I had had an intense curiosity over his choice of vehicles for his grueling around-the-world journey.

"Why," I asked, "are you using a nineteen-year-old vehicle for so demanding a venture?"

"Ed," he shot back, looking at me as if I were an annoying child, "the 1966 CJ-5 Jeep is the last vehicle of its kind to be made entirely in the United States, with all American parts and American labor. I'm one hundred percent American, and I'm going to go around the world in a one hundred percent American-made vehicle."

His reply was like a slap, but I saw it as a means for him to vent his frustrations. The bright red jeep with the yellow UPTON AND SON EXPEDITIONS logo emblazoned on the doors was not running well. Even the Isthmian Four-Wheeler Club mechanics were having problems adjusting the timing of the six-cylinder gasoline engine.

For several days Upton and the mechanics continued to work on his jeep, which he called the "S.S. Discovery." I made daily visits to witness the work, and I began to see another side of Upton that was as severe as his fixation with explorers and expeditions of the past. How complex a man I thought. He was driven by emotions that marked him as someone who set his own course and did not waver from it. The more I got to know him, the more my concern grew. Could our common goals offset the stresses we would find working our way through the Darien? And could we overcome the animosity that our negotiations had created?

Upton also had worries working on him. We both knew that crossing through the Panamanian side of the gap was a formidable challenge in itself. But the Colombians had set up what seemed to be an impregnable administrative barrier. The Colombian government had established Los Katíos, a national park adjacent to the border, hoping to preserve the fragile jungle environment and to insulate the Indians from corrupting outside influences. Since Upton's last passage through the gap, the Colombians had instituted a prohibition against motorized land vehicles of any kind within the park. The ban would help prevent the northward spread of *aftosa* — the hoof-and-mouth disease endemic to Colombian cattle.

Upton had already asked for permission to pass through the park, but the Colombians had refused and warned him not to attempt an entry. So I made another offer, this time to try to solve the Los Katíos problem.

I again turned to the Liskas. I asked Danny to intercede with the director of the Colombian park system to try to obtain permission for Upton's jeep and my Amigo to pass through the park. Liska declined, saying the director was adamant in his opposition to relaxing the park's vehicle prohibition.

Desperate, I made Upton another offer. I told him I would write to Malcolm Forbes, the magazine publisher and motorcycle enthusiast. I had previously invited Forbes to participate in or otherwise support my Darien Gap expedition. Now I asked him to apply his considerable influence to secure official permission for our vehicles to pass through the park. Much to Upton's disappointment, Forbes did not respond. And rightly so. The man did not know me personally, and he had no reason to involve himself directly in a project full of unknowns and in a setting reeking of potential controversies.

Los Katíos remained a problem. But having exhausted attempts to resolve it from Panama City, we decided to let it rest until we reached the border.

Our departure continued to meet delays. We were now faced with the start of Carnival, the pre-Lenten celebration that causes practically a week-long shutdown of official and commercial activity throughout the country. Panama became one great round of parades and parties. But for Upton and me the holiday meant we could not buy the last of the supplies and equipment we needed nor secure the official vehicle release documents from the customs office.

I rattled around aimlessly, not partaking in the festivities and regretting the wasted time — and money — that I could have used to ride Amigo down to Panama rather than flying. More importantly, I knew the dry season was well underway in the Darien. And every day we tarried meant fewer days of good weather in the jungle.

But Upton seemed unconcerned and even shaved time off his original estimate.

"Don't worry, Ed," he chided. "I'll have you in Bogotá well ahead of schedule. I guarantee it."

Upton's optimism sprang from his intention to employ the same Indian guides and follow the trails carved by the massive 1979 AMC Jeep expedition that had come up through the gap from Colombia. He planned to simply follow in reverse the broad path cut by the expedition.

Upton finally got his jeep tuned up and running smoothly. We made a test run of our vehicles out the Pipeline Road — a rough trail through the heavy undergrowth, hills and swampy ground paralleling the canal.

The path dated back to the 1940s when workers laid a wartime oil pipeline through the Canal Zone. Both Amigo and Discovery took the run in stride, and Upton declared us ready.

We finished our last-minute preparations. Pat Mercier started her leave from the Girl Scout office, and I bid farewell to my Road Knights hosts. Then early on February 21, a dry, bright morning, our slow-moving mini-convoy set out eastward on the Pan American Highway to go beyond the headwaters of the Chagres River, across the Bayano and along a path to hell.

6

Going Beyond the Chagres

Beyond the Chagres River,
'Tis said — the story's old —
Are paths that lead to mountains
Of purest virgin gold.
But 'tis my firm conviction,
Whatever tales they tell,
That beyond the Chagres River
All paths lead straight to hell!

James Stanley Gilbert
Panama Patchwork

Lawrence Upton and I rode on the motorcycle. Loren Upton had asked me — directed, actually — to ride two-up so he and Pat Mercier could jam themselves into the overloaded jeep.

"It's only temporary," Upton explained. "Once we cross thc Chucunaque River, I'll be the only one in the jeep. Lawrence and Pat will walk every step of the way through the Darien, out in front of the jeep, so they can work the winch and guide me through the tight spots."

Lawrence, a motocross rider himself, enjoyed the ride on Amigo. We passed the succession of rivers lying to the east of Panama City and skirted the hills that held the source of the Chagres River. As we approached the Bayano River, I took Lawrence on a detour to see the new Bayano Dam.

An alert Panamanian Defense Force guard nearly arrested us when he caught me taking pictures of the dam. After convincing the PDF guard of our innocent intentions, I found the incident amusing. In all my previous visits while the dam was being built, I had never once been challenged, although I had taken scores of photos from the foundations up to the sluice gates.

The dam had formed a lake thirty miles long, and Indians had built villages along the new shoreline. We crossed the lake on the same bridge I had watched being built ten years earlier. On each side of the road, distant lateral ranges of low mountains formed a wide corridor for the Pan Am. With the dry season at its height, the nearly cloudless morning sky was clear except for a slight haze of dust and smoke rising from Indian slash-and-burn jungle-clearing operations.

We stopped at Cañazas for gas, not knowing if there would be fuel available up ahead. We also had to check in with the PDF guard post at the entrance to the *Comarca,* the Darien's autonomous Indian region.

I was surprised at the changes that had taken place since I had ridden back to Panama City from Yaviza last year in Javier Tapia's truck. Opening the new section of

the Pan American Highway had brought a surge of immigration and development. We passed numerous
trucks and small buses that kicked up clouds of reddish
dust. And where thatched huts had stood before there
were now clapboard houses with corrugated roofs. At
Canglón I saw that Javier Tapia's house was finished.
But neither he nor Florencio, the motorcyclist, were
around. Their neighbors said they were up in the hills
behind the village tending their crops.

Just beyond Canglón, Lawrence and I caught up with
Upton and Pat. They had had to stop to get permission
from the road contractor's office to proceed along the
remaining twenty miles of new construction to Yaviza.
The road had still not officially opened, and we bumped
and rattled along the rutted, single track that had all
but been destroyed by the last rainy season.

Upton had to resort to using the jeep's four-wheel
drive. I was hard put to stay upright behind him at the
slow speed and with the top-heavy weight of Lawrence
to contend with. Unfortunately, following the jeep at a
crawling pace was an omen of times to come.

We bounced into Yaviza late in the afternoon, lurch-
ing onto the concrete sidewalk-wide street and paraded
down to the plaza. There Upton jumped from the jeep
and began issuing orders.

"Ed," he bellowed, "see about gasoline. And remember, we have to line up a piragua and crew to carry the
heavy gear. But don't pay too much for them! Lawrence,
you watch the jeep while Pat and I head for the missionary station to hire guides."

But before Upton could stride off too far, an unsmil-
ing PDF corporal confronted us, gruffly demanding to

see our papers. I sensed the soldier was intent on causing trouble. He showed none of the courtesy or friendly interest that I had experienced before with members of the Yaviza PDF contingent. So I did not even bother to produce my passport, but drew out the plastic-encased letter from General Noriega.

"Yo tengo algo más valioso," I said confidently, handing the soldier my far more impressive document.

The corporal started visibly as he saw the four gold stars embossed on the letterhead. He studied the text and then looked up with a chastened expression. He handed the letter back and saluted smartly. Now a model of obsequiousness, he excused himself while backing away and wished me good luck and a successful trip through the Darien.

Upton had witnessed the exchange and said, "I wasn't sure that letter was worth the paper it was written on until I saw that little PDF two-striper back off like he had been bitten by a bushmaster." Tapping the letter he added, "You'd better keep it safe and handy, because I guarantee you we'll need it again."

Upton and Pat left and I went off to carry out my tasks. I found a source of gasoline, which was still priced at four dollars per gallon. I also hired a piragua and crew to transport our excess gear. I visited the PDF headquarters, where I found the troops had already heard of our arrival, probably via the recently subdued corporal. The commander gave us permission to camp overnight at the PDF *bohio,* a thatched-roof gazebo on the high bank of the Chucunaque River. I asked about Sergeant Morales, whom I had met on last year's trip to Yaviza, but was disappointed to hear he was not there.

Upton and Pat had been gone for hours when they returned at sundown. Upton reported that he had arranged for a trail-cutting crew. He had lined up a mixed group of Panamanians and Indians, several of whom he had used in previous expeditions. He added that he had also hired a piragua and crew for the excess gear.

Despite his instructions to me before he left, Upton had duplicated the arrangements I had made with another piragua crew. This was my first experience with his erratic managerial style.

Upton's piragua crew — an Indian man and wife team — would carry our heavy equipment and extra gasoline. This supply piragua would follow us into the Darien Gap, but would stick to the rivers — the Chucunaque and then upriver on the Tuira. We planned to meet the couple at prearranged points to refuel and resupply.

It was dark by the time we set up camp at the PDF bohio. Our sleeping and eating arrangements were those we would use throughout the Darien venture. Upton unloaded a sectional table and bolted one side to the jeep. On the opposite side he screwed two legs into the base. We would use the table to eat on while standing around it. At night Upton made it his bed.

Pat slept inside the enclosed jeep, stretched out on cabinet-like food and equipment boxes Upton had built into the rear of the cab. Lawrence set up a conventional nylon tent on the ground and used a sleeping bag and air mattress. I slung my hammock between the bohio's roof supports.

Upton was up and out early the next morning. He was determined to get the jeep across the river immediately even though we had not yet completed all our preparations in Yaviza. He hired two additional piraguas, and we scoured the area for heavy planking with which to convert the canoes into a raft. Upton and Lawrence lashed the rough, hand-sawn planks on top of the piraguas, forming a platform just long and wide enough to support the jeep. The raft looked so frail and unsubstantial that I could not believe it would accommodate the jeep.

I should not have worried. Upton had done this before, and his only concern was to get the jeep aboard before the river fell any more. Yaviza sits beside a tidal estuary and the Chucunaque rises and falls as much as fifteen feet. Upton needed the high tide to be able to drive the jeep on and off the raft.

With the raft completed, Upton and Pat festooned Discovery with flags from countries he and the jeep had passed through since leaving Alaska. I moved about dutifully taking pictures. Then, following Lawrence's hand signals, Upton began to drive cautiously along the loading planks leading from the shore to the platform. But under the weight of the jeep the lumber buckled and then cracked with loud reports. Upton backed up the jeep, doubled the planks and Lawrence again guided him and the jeep along the ramp. This time the wood held, and he drove the jeep aboard the platform.

Upton ordered the boatman to start the outboard motor attached to one of the piraguas. The awkwardly handling raft slowly moved out into the river and across the hundred yards of water to a small depression in the opposite shore.

I watched as the jeep edged off the raft onto the

plank ramp. Suddenly Discovery tilted and lurched as the planks snapped again, violently rocking the piraguas and dropping the jeep. Upton gunned the engine to power the jeep up onto the bank where it disappeared into the jungle. He reappeared on foot, boarded the raft and came back to retrieve Pat, me and the motorcycle. We easily lifted Amigo onto the platform and in minutes were across the river, joining the rest of the expedition in a small clearing near where we landed.

We had made it across the Chucunaque — the first of three major river crossings and a score of fordings through shallower streams and creeks. But Upton introduced a disquieting note. He said he wasn't sure we had landed at the right spot. He could not positively identify the depression as the one that the 1979 AMC expedition had cut into the bank, and the one Upton had used on his trip through the Darien shortly afterwards.

If it was the right entry point, the relentless jungle had swallowed up the trail. We would have to hack another path through the gap, trying to recut the seven-year-old AMC trail. But that expedition had enjoyed lavish funding. They had a twenty-five-man platoon of Indians equipped with chain saws assigned solely to trail cutting.

Reportedly, the AMC expedition had paid over two hundred and fifty thousand dollars just to get through from Turbo in Colombia. Upton bitterly criticized the extravagance, blaming the AMC spending for our having to pay inflated wages of five to six dollars per day plus furnishing food for our eight-man crew.

We set up our first on-the-trail camp beside the river, and the next morning we began commuting via piragua

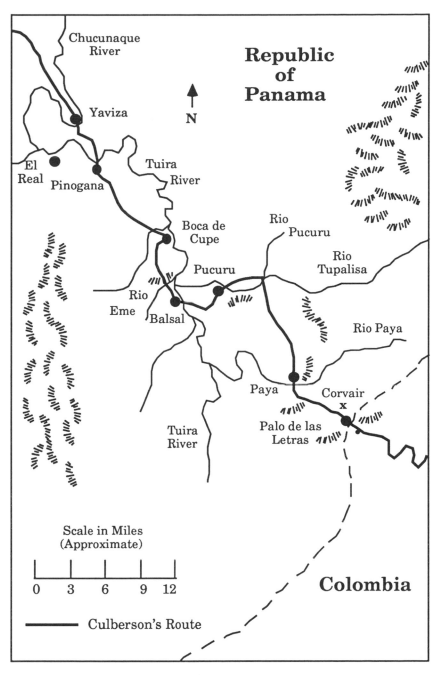

Darien Gap Area — Panama

between the camp and Yaviza to complete our preparations.

Upton directed Pat and me to buy a fifty-five-gallon drum of gasoline. At the local general store we watched as workers laboriously ladled the precious gasoline, gallon by four-dollar gallon, from smaller containers into the steel barrel. Pat and I supervised as the men awkwardly rolled the heavy drum down the Chucunaque's steep bank and hoisted it by hand into the rocking supply piragua. We next loaded parts for the jeep, a spare tire, our backpacks and extra food.

While Pat and I were in Yaviza, Upton and Lawrence scouted the trail we would take. Breaking in the crew Upton had recruited, they began to clear and widen the path.

We spent another night by the riverside, and the next morning we plunged into the thick vegetation. We were still close enough to civilization to navigate by the narrow footpaths the Indians used to get to their scattered plots of green, banana-like plantains. But these trails needed to be enlarged to accommodate the jeep and often they were blocked by downed trees.

I asked Upton why he hadn't brought along chain saws to cut through the fallen trees, whose diameters often ranged up to five and six feet. But my question again provoked his resentment of the AMC expedition.

"Goddammit, we're going to do this expedition the right way. The way it was meant to be done, with sweat, muscles and machetes. We're not doing it the easy way like that candy-ass AMC crowd."

His answer reflected his determination to make the expedition a test of his will against the strengths of the jungle. His stubborn, marine-like attitude meant the *macheteros,* the trail cutters, had to spend hours hacking away at the thick trees lying across the trail. They would usually make two cuts in the trees, one near each edge of the trail. When they had chopped through the trees in both spots, they pulled aside the middle section which blocked the trail. On larger trees Loren had to use the jeep's winch and cable to drag the sections aside.

Ravines cut by the rushing waters of the rainy season's heavy downpours also hampered our progress. Typically, the ravines were as much as ten feet deep and twice as wide, but occasionally we would come upon much deeper and wider cuts. Upton was in his element here, revelling in his role as expedition chief and drilling us in the art of winching the jeep out of the gullies.

He would first direct the crew in cutting back the bank's steep angle by digging away at its shoulders with shovels and machetes. Upton then got back behind the steering wheel and slowly edged the jeep over the bank and into the ravine. Lawrence would run the jeep's winch cable up the far side to secure it to a sturdy tree. When Upton engaged the winch, Lawrence would guide the cable back onto the winch roller, and the jeep would gradually pull itself out of the ravine.

I usually rode behind the jeep and could occasionally make it across the ravines on my own. But most were too narrow and steep-sided to get Amigo out under its own power. So I simply fell in behind Discovery, hooking onto the jeep's rear bumper with a light wire cable and harness attached to Amigo's frame. As Upton winched the jeep up the far side, I would hold the bike upright while Discovery towed Amigo along behind it.

When the Indian trails were identifiable and ran in the right direction, I would ride out ahead of the jeep. But this was seldom worthwhile. Inevitably, a downed tree or deep ravine would stop Amigo, and I would have to wait until the main party caught up with me. Sometimes I would take a wrong turn where a faint trail forked and would have to backtrack to find the main party.

It was slow going, but our plodding progress did not appear to worry Upton. "I don't want the trail to be too easy," he said. He was obviously enjoying the constant hacking through the vegetation and winching in and out of the ravines. He also remarked, "This is child's play compared to the much rougher terrain ahead."

Two days after setting out from Yaviza, we had hacked through four miles of jungle to reach the Tuira River, which we had to cross to reach the village of Pinogana on the opposite bank. Upton again hired two piraguas and built a platform on top of them to take the jeep and Amigo.

In Pinogana we bargained for more gasoline, and I created quite a stir with Amigo. Most of the children had never seen a motorcycle before. They were too young to have encountered Webb and Merrill on their Rokons. The children gleefully chased me up and down the village's dirt street, and I was able to gear up to second and third for the first time since leaving Yaviza.

Leaving Pinogana we followed a wide, deeply rutted trail that had been cut by a bulldozer in an attempt to link Pinogana with Boca de Cupe, La Palma and El Real. The road was never finished, and the abandoned hulk of the bulldozer lay rusting on the riverbank in

Pinogana. But the ruts it had left were treacherous. They were still filled with water from the rainy season which masked a sticky, red clay below. When I tried to ride through one, Amigo sank into the muck over its axles. I had to wait for Loren Upton and the jeep to drag me out of the quagmire. What, I wondered, would this route be like during the height of the wet season?

In the near week we took to cover the nine miles between Pinogana and Boca de Cupe, the trail continued to provide a cram course in enduro riding — jungle style. Amigo and I were taking some heavy hits. I bloodied my nose and broke the lens out of my eyeglasses when a tree branch caught me in the face. Amigo's left cylinder started misfiring, and the bike suffered a smashed right exhaust header pipe after hitting a concealed rock. We crashed often, and I would sweat profusely as I struggled to get Amigo and myself back on the trail. At times I felt dangerously close to heat exhaustion.

I forced myself to eat and drink enough to offset the fearsome heat-induced bodily stresses. Our diet had so far been adequate. For breakfast we usually had oatmeal sprinkled with raisins and whatever other fruit was available. The mid-day and supper staple was the now-monotonous beans and rice, which we tried to liven up with canned tuna or local foodstuffs such as plantains, yucca and manioc. For bread, the cooks fried lumps of dough in cooking oil to come up with *patacones* — duck's feet — which were our favorite while the flour and oil stocks lasted.

Loren Upton was a tea drinker, so our standard meal-time drink was honey-sweetened mugs of warm tea. When we ran out of the natural flavoring, we reverted to the dirty-looking unrefined local sugar.

On the tenth day of the expedition we approached the Cupe River and set up camp. We were within walking distance of the village of Boca de Cupe, the last real Panamanian village in the eastern Darien. The settlements remaining between Boca de Cupe and the Colombian border belonged exclusively to the Indians who maintain their own governmental authority. So we visited Boca de Cupe's storekeeper, *Don* Antonio, who also served as a consular officer, and had exit visas stamped in our passports.

While in the area of Boca de Cupe we added another member to our party, a young Frenchman named Harold Frebet. A lean, earnest adventurer, Frebet had reached Boca de Cupe on foot in the course of a seven-year-long journey around the world by walking or hitchhiking on any means of transportation available. Frebet had asked to join our expedition, fearing for his life in the dangerous environment of the Darien where solitary travelers are easy prey for predators — both human and animal. I was surprised that Upton agreed, which he did without consulting me or the others.

We got an early-morning start from our Boca de Cupe campsite, riding fast along clearly defined trails connecting farm plots and scattered thatched-roofed huts. But beyond the cultivated areas the broad trail narrowed and at times disappeared as we moved into rougher terrain.

I developed a hatred for the bamboo and plantain stalks left on the trail by the macheteros clearing our path. The debris had a slick and greasy surface. If I rode over the cuttings going uphill or riding along a slope, I would instantly spill as Amigo's wheels lost traction and slid out from under me.

Even worse were the tree stumps, cleverly disguised by nature to appear as clumps of innocent foliage. Fast-growing, flowering shoots issued from the stumps and hid the rock-solid interior. When Amigo's protruding cylinder guards slammed into the stumps the bike came to a bone-jarring stop, and I would pitch forward into the handlebars or even be thrown over the front end. The encounters would leave me bruised, and they eventually bent back Amigo's crash bars into the rocker covers of the cylinder heads.

Until now the land had been relatively flat, but low hills began to close in on each side of us. The terrain forced Upton to winch more often. And on occasion he had to use what he called a "comealong," a hand-operated winch, to secure the jeep from the side to keep it from rolling over on some of the steep slopes.

I became impatient with the slower pace, obliged to dawdle behind the jeep and watch as Lawrence and Loren worked the now-familiar routine of anchoring the tow rope to a carefully selected tree, Lawrence guiding the cable as it was drawn back over the winch drum, and the jeep slowly moving forward up the steep hills and ravines.

Pat Mercier had supplanted me as team photographer. She was quietly competent in this role as she was in her other duties. Pat maintained watch over the supplies and equipment, helped supervise the Indian cooks and buffered Upton's increasingly frequent displays of imperious anger. Her presence had a restraining effect on us all that was totally without sexual overtones. She was simply a rock-solid member of the crew who became more indispensable as the trail got rougher.

Lawrence, despite his youth, also showed remarkable composure in the face of Upton's sometimes unreasonable requirements. He was always willing to respond to the toughest tasks, and never once did I see him lose his temper or rebel against the sometimes-onerous duties Upton assigned him.

My tactic was to keep my distance, to maintain a reserve against the overwhelming domination that Upton, consciously or not, exerted at every opportunity. He took on a more pronounced authoritarian role now that we were solidly in his element and under his sole control. But I could not always accept his arbitrary decisions. And he criticized me for it.

"Ed," he asked during a placid moment, "how is it that you're really not a member of the team, that you seem to have set yourself apart and have never become one of us?"

"But Loren, Pat has now become your photographer, and you no longer need me as an interpreter," I replied, referring to when he had fired our supply piragua crew. After that incident, Upton never again asked me to translate for him.

He had become dissatisfied with the work of the Indian couple he had hired for the supply piragua, and he wanted to discharge them. He brought me along to translate as he paid them off and sent them back to Yaviza. But the Indians disputed the amount of money owed them. Their halting, primitive Spanish was hard to translate, and Upton became impatient over the slow exchange. He took over using his few words of pidgin Spanish. His vocabulary was totally inadequate, but his anger was unmistakable in any language as he furiously counted out the amount he calculated was due them. He threw the money down and declared, "I am absolutely and totally correct in this matter." Ignoring the protests of the Indians, he stalked away.

Upton and I also had different priorities. He expected me to devote my full attention to advancing the jeep on the trail, as he did of Lawrence, Pat and now Harold Frebet. He believed that nothing else, especially Amigo, should take higher precedence in our activities. The strain increased when the broad footpad on Amigo's sidestand broke off. I had no choice but to either hold the bike upright when I stopped or look for a tree to lean Amigo against. Consequently, I could not immediately respond to Upton's demands for assistance with the jeep. Later, I fashioned a stout Y-shaped tree branch into a makeshift sidestand, but it took time to rig up whenever I stopped — more time than Upton allowed when he called for help with the jeep.

Upton obviously did not understand my deep attachment to my bike, a tie that is typical of most serious motorcyclists. Upton had been a horseman, and surely he must have developed a close bond between himself and the animals he rode. Did he not realize that Amigo was my horse, my reason for being there? I could not subordinate my attentions to Amigo in favor of the jeep.

Our rising personal differences were soon overshadowed by bigger problems on our march to the next landmark — a small creek called the Rio Eme. Since leaving Boca de Cupe we had spent days trying to confirm that we were on the right track, desperately looking for faint clues that we were following the AMC trail. The relentless growth of lush vegetation, which had grown thicker again as we moved into the hills, had obliterated practically all traces of the trail.

Trying to detect the path became sort of a game. We looked for ranks of trees that were less than seven years old. On hills we examined stands of stout, older trees for barely visible circular scars left in the bark by winch cables. We also checked stumps, branches and exposed roots for chain saw-cut straight surfaces Even the guides who had worked for the AMC group and had accompanied Upton on his 1979 expedition were unsure of the route. At one point Loren had to hire two new guides who claimed they knew the way to the border.

But no matter how difficult the going, Upton was meticulous in his journal keeping. He faithfully recorded every act and incident in his notebooks as it happened or immediately thereafter. Lawrence, Harold and I felt sure that he even noted the exact time, location, color, consistency and quantity of each of his bowel movements while in the jungle.

When we reached the Rio Eme we were confronted by a formidable obstacle. We had to cross a steep-sided ravine that dropped about 160 feet down to a narrow, rock-filled stream bed. Crossing the shallow creek itself would be easy. But the descent along the near-vertical bluff, and the climb up the almost equally steep hill on the opposite bank, would be a real test of Loren's skill and ingenuity.

Upton reversed the jeep in the heavy underbrush

and backed it to the edge of the hill. Lawrence rigged the winch cable to a massive tree, and Loren cautiously backed Discovery over the edge, letting the winch slowly pay out the cable as the jeep moved down, its nose pointing to the sky. The taut cable sliced into the edge of the bluff as it took the full weight of the jeep.

Twice Upton let the winch unwind almost the entire cable. Then he stopped while Lawrence anchored the jeep with other cables. Upton would rewind the winch cable, and Lawrence would rig it to a tree close by so the snail-like descent could start again.

Suddenly, seventy feet down the bank, Upton shouted, "We're losing oil pressure! I've got to shut it down!" Without a steady flow of oil the engine would quickly overheat and seize.

With the jeep pointing precariously upward, Lawrence frantically secured it with extra cables. Upton said he thought Discovery's near-vertical position on the steep embankment was drawing the oil away from the pressure sensor. Gambling that the engine had enough oil flowing despite the warning light, he decided to resume the descent.

He had difficulty restarting the engine, but when he did the motor ran so roughly it did not have enough power to operate the winch. He shut it down again. Upton got out of the jeep and inspected the motor. He discovered the problem was far worse than he had imagined. The engine was rapidly losing oil.

He resorted to using the comealong, the hand-operated winch. I could not believe that this jack-like device was strong enough to anchor the jeep in place, much less allow it to move safely down the slope. But

Loren assured me it had a rated capacity more than equal to the task. Still, we struggled for six and a half hours to lower Discovery the remaining ninety feet to the bottom of the creek bed.

With the jeep back in a horizontal position, Upton again examined the engine. He confirmed that the steep, backward descent had not caused the oil loss — the engine had a leaking main oil seal. We were facing a major mechanical breakdown in the most remote area the expedition had reached so far. Trapped by the steeply rising banks on each side of the valley, we were virtual prisoners of the Rio Eme. Thank God no rain was in sight, or we would be caught up in the roaring flood waters that inundate the narrow valley.

We would remain imprisoned here for four more days, sentenced to hard labor to gain our release. We were literally at the low point of the expedition, and Lawrence Upton came up with a fitting description of our plight.

"Do you know what *Eme*" — the letter *m* in Spanish — "stands for?" he asked. "It stands for *mierda,* Spanish for shit. And that's a good name for this place. We're up Shit Creek!"

7

Thirty-Three Days to Defeat

*Expeditions generate antipathies
and jungles inspire tensions;
marry the one to the other
and the honeymoon will be brief.*

Russell Braddon
The Hundred Days of Darien

A lthough he had no replacement oil seal on hand, Upton refused to even consider abandoning the jeep. He decided to try overpowering the leak by adding more oil than the engine was throwing out. He hoped to keep the oil flowing in the engine long enough to winch out of the ravine. Once he had the jeep on level ground, Upton thought it would lose less oil.

Lawrence secured the winch cable to a tree midway up the slope and poured the last of the expedition's oil into the jeep's crankcase. Slowly, Loren Upton began to winch the jeep up the steep hill. But after only fifteen feet the engine again ran low on oil. Upton tied off the jeep and dispatched Lawrence and Harold back to Boca de Cupe — or further if necessary — to buy a case of engine oil. Loren, Pat and I stayed with the jeep, now anchored precariously upward on the Rio Eme's other bank.

I found the interlude frustrating. I marked time by doing my laundry, soaping down my clothes in the tranquil creek waters and hanging them out to catch the rays of the midday sun that filtered down through the overhanging vegetation. This was the only direct sunlight we were able to see.

The next day Lawrence and Harold returned with a case of oil. Upton filled the crankcase and set about the job of again winching the jeep. But the engine, straining mightily under the jeep's weight and the pull up the sheer slope, leaked oil copiously. Upton had to again cut the engine.

He decided to try the comealong. He hooked up the hand winch and cable and began the push-pull on the handle required to work the jack. But the gear teeth were so worn that the ratchet dogs would engage only the last few teeth, reducing the upward drawing distance to what Lawrence calculated as only one-half inch per pull!

It was exhausting, discouraging, sweat-drenching toil. We all took turns pushing and pulling the comealong's handle. I would last only a few minutes before having to give up panting, completely drained. Loren, Lawrence and the Panamanian guides did the most frequent shifts.

On the third day they began right after breakfast, straining continuously from eight o'clock until late afternoon. The two Uptons and the more hardy of the Panamanians took turns working the jack. In seven hours of absolutely wretched, hand-blistering drudgery, including twenty-seven changes in comealong and tie-off cable positions, they succeeded in moving the jeep uphill a total of 105 feet.

We tried to psychologically offset the heavy physical toil and keep morale up by naming our river-bottom campsite "Camp Mishap," and the eastern bank "Misery Hill." Loren repeatedly referred to our predicament as romantic high adventure. I had a problem seeing anything at all romantic about our situation.

Our attempts at reverse psychology took a beating when we discovered a rusting, faded sign nailed to a tree on the hillside. Almost illegible, it proclaimed the midway point for the 1979 AMC Jeep expedition. Although the sign was rare confirmation that we were on the projected route of the Pan American Highway, it raised a disquieting question. Did the sign mark the half-way point of the entire AMC expedition between Cape Horn and Alaska or only the mid-point through the Darien Gap? If it was the latter, it meant that we had been on the trail for three weeks and were still not even close to the end of our trek.

Relief from those dark thoughts came early on the fifth day when the comealong, now with ratchet teeth so worn each pull moved Discovery only one-quarter inch upward, brought the jeep slowly to the crest of the cliff and onto fairly level ground. I followed with Amigo, holding the bike upright while the rest of the crew pulled it uphill using a rope and pulley.

Upton again checked the jeep engine's rate of oil loss and concluded that the leak would not hinder driving to the next village. He was right and for the next two days we slowly limped the last few miles to Balsal, a small Choco Indian village on a bank of the Tuira River.

Balsal was unlike any other village we had seen. The Choco, a much smaller tribe than the Darien's dominant Cuna Indians, were friendly and generous. The chief — more an honorary title than a meaningful position among the casual Choco — invited us to share his sleeping house, a rickety, wooden clapboard structure built on wood stilts. An inclined tree trunk with steps carved in it lead to the elevated home where the chief lived with his family. A menagerie of perpetually noisy animals occupied the ground below.

That night the noise of the animals disturbed our pleasure at sleeping on a firm, dry surface. One large dog in particular resented our intrusion and spent the entire night barking in protest. Our only respite from the animals came when our minds would shift to the hordes of cockroaches swarming in the darkness. I blessed the protective built-in mosquito netting of my jungle hammock which I had strung from the rafters, much to the envy of the others.

The next day, while Upton worked on the jeep, I idled about, watching the chief's wife and daughter working in the cooking pavilion. We had bargained for two meals a day for a dollar and were rewarded by a plate of beans, rice and plantains for breakfast.

On our arrival, I had been surprised to see a three-foot-wide concrete sidewalk running practically the entire two-block length of the village. Sidewalks were not a standard civic improvement for jungle villages, and I wondered how it had gotten there. The chief answered my question.

"*Muchos años* — many years ago," he said in his carefully enunciated Spanish, "the great *jefe* of the republic came here to visit. It was the first time we had ever seen a *jefe* from Panama City here in Balsal.

"He came in a big, noisy bird" — the Indian indicated a helicopter by waving his hands in a circular pattern — "and walked around our village. But it had rained, and the great general soiled his bright, shiny boots in the red mud of our poor village. He was angry and said, 'This must not be.'

"A few days after he flew away, many piraguas came here from Boca de Cupe and Yaviza carrying bags of cement. And we fashioned the sidewalk you now see, so that we do not have to walk in the mud during the rains."

I knew right away which great chief he was talking about, and it sure as hell wasn't General Noriega. The chief led me down the sidewalk to a small square. Here the grateful residents of Balsal had erected a crude silhouetted profile of General Omar Torrijos.

It was typical of Torrijos that he would visit a remote village such as Balsal. A populist and well-regarded leader, he allied himself closely with the Panamanian people and extended his concern to the isolated Indian tribes. During his time in power, billboards throughout the republic proclaimed his slogan: "What I want for my sons, I want for Panama!"

To thank the chief, I took him on a motorcycle ride up and down the sidewalk, much to his pleasure and the amusement of the other villagers. The chief had a daughter about fifteen years old who had never before seen a motorcycle, and I asked him if his daughter would also like a ride. He approved and she agreed, but not before she ran to the sleeping house to prepare for her big adventure.

Choco women go topless — the men are almost bottomless, wearing only a brief loincloth. And when the chief's daughter came out of the house she had changed into another, more elaborate skirt and had put on an absolutely stunning array of gold and silver jewelry. As modestly as I could I examined the necklaces which almost obscured her breasts. What appeared to be Spanish doubloons and pieces of eight dangled from the heavy chains. Other chains held *huacas* — ancient Indian gold figurines which were much sought after by Darien grave robbers.

The girl was not putting on a vain display. She was simply responding to a visitor's invitation by dressing up for what would probably be a once-in-a-lifetime ride. And as the chief's only daughter, the girl proudly wore the family jewels — the treasures that might well predate even the Balboa era and had been passed down through generations of this Choco family.

I invited the girl to mount the motorcycle behind me, and I made another tour of Balsal. With the girl clinging to me tightly, we rolled down the sidewalk and bounced off the concrete into the dirt to turn around. She made a disturbingly sensual impression on me, which lasted only until just after the ride. Flushed with delight, the girl's reserved Mona Lisa smile broadened to reveal that she had no front teeth. Like many of the Darien Indians, she had undoubtedly lost them by chewing on the raw sugar cane that substitutes for commercially produced sweets which are not available in the jungle.

Supper that evening was much the same as breakfast. The chief's wife prepared beans, rice and plantains but with the addition of a small chunk of meat, our first since leaving Boca de Cupe. The meat was stringy and seemed tougher than a football. I wondered about it. It didn't taste like the wild pig we had heard grunting and snarling in the forest. And it certainly wasn't the far more tender iguana or the diminutive *paca*, a rodent-like animal I knew the Indians favored.

Before I could ask the chief, it hit me. Since morning I had not heard one bark out of that damned dog that had shattered the nighttime jungle tranquility. Apparently the chief had been annoyed also. But even after two tours in Korea, where dog meat is commonly eaten, I was not prepared for the conclusion that I had again enlarged my eating experiences. I entertained thoughts of becoming a vegetarian.

Our restive pause and the pleasant distractions ended the next day when Upton declared the jeep ready. I don't know what miracle he performed to repair the oil leak. He had asked for neither advice nor help, but he and Lawrence had accomplished the task. He now supervised construction of a sturdy log raft large enough to float both the jeep and Amigo across the Tuira River.

We navigated the placid Tuira easily, but debarking on the far shore was tough. The bank was a sharply angled, fifteen-foot slope of slippery mud. Drawing the jeep directly from the raft up the bank was a tricky winch job, and Upton constantly ordered new angles for the tow cables to reduce the strain on the tree anchors, pulleys and winch roller.

I could not use my usual tactic of hooking Amigo to the rear of the jeep with my towing bridle. Only after the jeep reached more level ground and was secured could I go to work on Amigo. I tied ropes to the towing harness, and we used a pulley to drag the bike up the muddy bank. The exhausting job took the raw muscle power of the entire party. The struggle left me filthy, breathing hard and drenched in sweat from the exertion.

"Just you wait until we get up there," Upton said pointing ominously eastward to the hills ahead of us. "You'll really see what tough pulls are like."

Although Upton may not have meant it as such, I felt his remark was a rebuke, a reflection of my preoccupation with Amigo and a lesser regard for the jeep. We still had not come to terms with our individual priorities on the expedition. I still felt that being part of the jeep crew was not my primary responsibility. It was Amigo that would get me to Bogotá, and the motorcycle deserved my first concern.

We camped for the night on the river bank. I slept restlessly. The rift between Upton and me continued to widen and was just about irreparable. We had about six miles to go to reach Pucuru, and I decided to see how I could manage by myself. I would hire a team of Indians and break away from the Upton party to head for Pucuru on my own.

The next morning I told Upton of my intention. He seemed not at all surprised, but I did detect an unspoken feeling of concern. We agreed to meet at Pucuru, and I set about lining up a crew to help me.

Apparently the "jungle telegraph" had been at work, for a delegation of Cuna Indians had come out from their village at Pucuru to supervise our entry into their tribal territory. One of the men was Francisco Garrido, whom I had met earlier in Boca de Cupe. A soft-spoken, middle-aged man, he was the *corregidor* of Pucuru — the village chief. He and his brother, Enrique, agreed to help me. Francisco said it would be an easy walk to Pucuru. But he had never broken trail for a motorcycle before, and his estimate was woefully wrong.

We had trouble right from the start. Just trying to ride Amigo up the slope leading from the riverbank turned into a disheartening battle. Amigo's right cylinder was still misfiring. With my pitifully inadequate mechanical skills I hadn't realized it at the time, but the spark plug wire had broken.

I would start off with full throttle, but the crippled cylinder still sputtered. Then the wire would arc and the plug would suddenly cut in, overwhelming me with a sudden burst of full power. To make the situation worse, the leaves that covered the inclined trail were slick with morning dew. I could not get enough of a running start, and Amigo repeatedly stalled and fell over. The bike and I would then tumble backward down the steep incline.

Banged and bruised after six attempts, I finally admitted I could not ride the bike up to the crest, and we resorted to the bridle and tow rope. Francisco and Enrique dragged the motorcycle by hauling on the rope while I stumbled upward beside Amigo, holding the bike upright with my hip against the seat and using the motor by slipping the clutch in and out to assist the straining Indians.

We would use this system again and again. But we encountered several hills where our teamwork was only just barely able to overcome the steep slopes. I needed a pulley to use with the rope, which would then double the muscle power of the two Indians. I sent Enrique to Upton with a note asking him to loan me a pulley. When the Indian returned, he had a pulley and a note from Upton:

> Am I feeding something tame and then turning it loose to forage for itself in the wilds! Ed — the hills get bigger up front! Then what, when there is no rope....Ed please be careful and not do something without considering, if not your own well being, then the pain that may be in and from your family — God be with you!

I had not expected Loren's display of concern, and I was deeply moved. I was also grateful for the pulley which made our work on the hills much easier. But shortly, Upton sent Harold Frebet to ask for return of the pulley. Upton needed it himself, as I well knew. I sent the pulley back, verbally beating myself about the head and shoulders for not having brought one of my own.

That ended our march for the day. I parked Amigo against a tree, collected my gear and set out walking to Pucuru. Francisco and Enrique led the way as I scouted the trail for tomorrow's ride.

We were only a few miles from their village, and soon we began following distinct footpaths that linked plots of cultivated land cut or burned out of the undergrowth. In one still-smouldering area, Francisco confessed that his villagers had let a small fire get out of control, burning far more land than they needed for their crops.

When we reached Pucuru, Francisco "invited" me to stay in his stilt house in an upper-level room which was set aside for visitors. He said I would pay one dollar per day for the sleeping room — which would be shared with any other visitors who might happen by — and another dollar for food cooked in the earthen-floored kitchen below.

As the head of the village, a position to which he was elected by the adult males, Francisco was responsible for maintaining the strict tribal customs. The democratic Cuna formed much closer-knit, more highly organized groups than the easier-going Choco tribe. Not too many years ago outsiders were not permitted to remain overnight in Cuna settlements. Now visitors were accepted only with the consent of the chief and if necessary with confirmation from the males of the tribe.

The next morning, after an early breakfast, Francisco, Enrique and I hiked back to Amigo. I had not lost any sleep over the thought of leaving the bike in the jungle overnight. Nobody was about to steal it, and there was nothing left on it to dismantle. I found the bike just as I left it — resting against the tree, looking forlorn and terribly out of place.

We wasted no time getting back to work. We sorely missed the pulley, but it seemed that with practice we were getting better wrestling Amigo up the hills.

I was at the bottom of one hill, preparing to ride Amigo up a long slope, when Francisco and Enrique began shouting frantically, *"Vispas, vispas!"* Killer bees — Africanized bees whose aggressive attacks in swarms earned them their nickname. They had attacked before when I was with Upton. But it was usually the *macheteros* out front, or Lawrence Upton when he attached winch cables to trees containing their nests, who suffered the attacks.

This time I was the point man, and I found that the sound of the motorcycle engine seemed to enrage the bees, drawing them out in angry waves. In panic, I dropped the bike and scrambled up the hill swatting at the swarm buzzing around my helmet. Nearing the crest of the hill I felt several stabs of pain as some of the bees succeeded in their attack. I threw myself over the crest but landed awkwardly on my left ankle. As it twisted, I felt the familiar shock of a sprain in my chronically weak Paratrooper ankle.

Mercifully, the bees retreated, leaving me swearing in pain. I limped back to the downed motorcycle and stifled a grunt as I picked it up. With Francisco and Enrique leading the way, we quietly walked Amigo along the side of the hill, away from the bees. Then I quickly rode the bike up to the crest, ready to outrun another attack if necessary.

While I was nursing my swelling ankle, Francisco launched a retaliatory strike against the bees. He chopped down a bamboo pole, gathered dried leaves and palm fronds and fashioned a torch. Stealthily, he carried it to the tree holding the hive. Francisco quickly lit the torch and held it up underneath the hive to let the flames and smoke envelope it. He said only a few of the bees escaped.

Like all the Darien's Indians, Francisco had come to hate the African strain of bees which had migrated north from Brazil. The Darien was not a barrier for the bees, as it was to the ground-level spread of the hoof-and-mouth disease common in Colombian cattle. The invading bees had quickly decimated the more tranquil domestic varieties, greatly reducing honey supplies and terrorizing the Indians with their sometimes-fatal swarming attacks.

My ankle injury was painful but not disabling. We were only a few miles from Pucuru, and I was able to ride much of the way. Once back in the village, I again set up in Francisco's house.

I was fortunate to have been befriended by Francisco and Enrique. They made my next few days a pleasant interlude that helped buffer an exhaustion of mind and body that threatened to do me in. The respite also allowed my ankle to mend. But most of all, my stay in Pucuru let me assess my situation and to rein in a sense of despair that was beginning to rise within me.

8

Back From the Gap

Not in the clamor of the crowded street,
Not in the shouts and plaudits of the throng,
But in ourselves, are triumph and defeat.

Longfellow
The Poets

I had made the six miles from the Tuira River in two days, covering more distance than we had in the preceding two weeks. But I couldn't go further until Upton caught up and brought my gear, and it would be several days at least before he would arrive in Pucuru.

I gimped around the village on my sore and swollen

ankle, taking a closer look at the Cuna culture. Pucuru was an orderly collection of about thirty-five thatched-roof, clapboard-sided houses, mostly built on stilts that varied in height from one house to the next. The village also had two more-elaborate houses with corrugated metal roofs, one at each end of the dirt street. These belonged to missionaries, two American couples who were away on vacation.

Francisco invited me to scout the trail to Paya, the next village. He said there was only one possible route eastward, and I would have to take it to get to Colombia. I wrapped my ankle tightly with an elastic bandage from my first aid kit and found I could walk in reasonable comfort.

Francisco and I left the village and waded easily through the shallow Pucuru River. I made a mental note of the route, calculating how I would get Amigo through the river and up the low bank. Along the trail to Paya Francisco showed considerable civic pride. He said the path, which was wide enough for us to walk abreast, was a cooperative effort. During each dry season all able members of the Pucuru tribe went out in work parties to clear the trail. They cut back the encroaching brush and hacked through the trees that had fallen across the path.

Shortly after leaving Pucuru the trail curved upward steeply yet smoothly along an increasingly precarious escarpment overlooking the Pucuru River. Francisco watched me peer cautiously down the cliff and confirmed my fears.

"Yes, it's very dangerous," he said.

Each year the bank becomes more unstable as it

erodes, and the Indians have to shift the trail away from the precipice. I have to remember this, I thought, and warn Loren Upton of the danger of the ground breaking away under the weight of the jeep.

Several miles later we angled down from a ridge to the confluence of the Pucuru and Tupalisa rivers. The river junction marked the end of Francisco's jurisdiction. Beyond here the Cuna tribe from Paya maintained the trail.

We paused for a while along the river bank. I took off my boots and bandage and dangled my fat ankle in the cooling waters. I found Francisco to be a most agreeable companion and guide. He belied the Cuna reputation for aloofness. Perhaps it was our comparable ages that had led to an unspoken, mutual regard that began back on the trail from Balsal. As we sat, Francisco told me of an incident that happened three years ago.

At this very place he had found the carcass of a mule wedged against the rocks in the river. He found out later that the animal belonged to a Costa Rican — an itinerant writer and poet named Helirueda who had spent years wandering around South America. He had decided to return to his birthplace and had entered Panama from Colombia. He reached Paya, and then set out for Pucuru. But he never made it and disappeared without a trace somewhere along this route. Only his mule had been found.

Francisco said it was very mysterious. The Costa Rican could have drowned trying to cross the river which was extremely turbulent during the rainy season. But more likely he had been set upon by robbers and killed for whatever valuables he may have had. They probably dragged his body off the trail and into the jungle for natural predators to dispose of. The mule, too obvious to be of value to the robbers, was probably let loose to drown in the raging river.

I recognized Francisco's story for what it was — a gentle warning about the dangers lurking in the Darien. But what concerned me even more at the moment were the dark, vaporous clouds building up over the hills toward Paya. I could even hear the faint, ominous rumble of thunder. The Darien's dry season was in its final days.

From what I had seen of the trail so far, it would be easy to reach Paya, with or without Upton and the jeep. But beyond Paya, the cleared, well-kept trail ended. And I would find only more precipitous hills, higher ridges and deeper ravines to struggle over and through to reach Palo de las Letras, the small monument marking the Panamanian-Colombian border. Beyond the crest of the divide that separates the two countries I would encounter obstacles that would loom even more serious if the rains started.

Francisco noted my apprehensive glances at the sky. "Yes," he said, "the rains will be here shortly. You will not be able to get through."

When the rains came the trail would turn treacherous. The rushing, rain-swollen rivers would be imposible to cross. Francisco had verified for me what I had already concluded — I was not going to reach the Colombian border and beyond this year.

On the way back to Pucuru, trudging dejectedly alongside Francisco, I told him of my decision. As soon as Loren Upton and the expedition arrived I would recover my gear and return to Panama, taking Amigo downriver by piragua. Francisco seemed relieved.

"But what will the others do?" he asked.

I told him I didn't know, but I expected that Upton would stubbornly press on despite the deteriorating weather which was already pelting Francisco and me with scattered raindrops. Upton had pledged more than once never to take one step backwards in his around-the-world quest. He would stay in the jungle throughout the rainy season if necessary. By the time he reached Pucuru he would probably need a resupply of food and gas, which would take days to bring upriver. He had to stop. The only question was when and where.

I had heard some Cuna say that Upton would not be allowed to stay in Pucuru. Other rumors said he would be charged an exorbitant fee to bring the jeep into the village and to stay there, but the Cuna would not permit Upton's Panamanian crew members to remain for long in Pucuru. They would have to be replaced by Indians, a requirement that Upton would surely balk at.

The next day Harold Frebet, scouting ahead of the main party, arrived at Pucuru. He told me that on the trail someone had said the villagers of Pucuru would charge Upton one hundred dollars per day to broaden the trail to Paya for the jeep. The jungle telegraph was clattering madly. I wondered if the swirl of Upton rumors resulted from his previous passage along this route.

The day following Harold's arrival, the thirty-first since we had left Yaviza, the expedition arrived in Pucuru. Upton was at the wheel of the flag-bedecked jeep, and the others walked escort beside him. They paraded slowly down the unpaved street as the villagers watched attentively. The jeep was the first four-wheeled motor vehicle to arrive at the village in over seven years. It was a new experience for the youngsters and a festive occasion for the adults.

Even so, the Cuna had to decide how to officially respond to the Upton party. With repeated blasts on a trumpet made from a wild boar tusk, Francisco summoned all adult males to the meeting house. Loren Upton and Pat Mercier were permitted to attend but were not allowed to take part in the proceedings. That Pat could sit in was an extraordinary relaxation of the Cuna's tradition against women participating in communal deliberations. I chose not to attend. Whatever the Cuna decided would not affect me.

After the meeting Pat told me that Francisco and the villagers would allow Upton and the jeep to stay in Pucuru, and he would only have to pay the same small fees that I had been charged. I was glad Upton had not been confronted with extravagant demands. Surely he would have angrily rejected them, even though he was not in a position to bargain.

Upton was obviously suffering the same frustrations and sense of failure that I felt. He appeared gaunt and haggard from the exertions of the past month, and he had also hurt his leg. He didn't need a confrontation.

Relieved at being permitted to stay in Pucuru, Upton began scouting for a site on which he could store the jeep and build a shelter for himself. He refused to consider leaving the jeep even for a brief return to the outside world. He was adamant. He would wait out the rains in Pucuru. Pat, Lawrence and Harold, however, were preparing for their return to Panama City.

I left early the next morning, before the others, and our farewells were brief and unemotional. Loren and I had little left to say except to bid each other good fortune and to wordlessly salute the one thing we had left in common — our obsession to conquer the Darien, each in his own way.

Francisco arranged for me to ride downriver with Enrique and his helper Santiago. Lawrence Upton saw me off at the riverside, and I could tell that he too was suffering the regret of not having reached our goal. Lawrence and I lifted Amigo on board Enrique's piragua. Amigo's wide, opposed-piston cylinders neatly balanced the cycle in the narrow craft. I had removed Amigo's seat and nearly-empty gas tank to lower the bike's center of gravity, and we found that the outriggers Enrique had installed were not really necessary.

Enrique started us off by poling downriver, but the Pucuru's water level was so low that the piragua was continually grounding on the rocky bottom. We had to repeatedly jump out and push the canoe through the shallows. When we intersected the broader, deeper Tuira River, Enrique and Santiago switched to paddles.

As the piragua sliced smoothly through the waters of the Tuira, I looked back upstream, in the direction of the Rio Eme and the village of Balsal. The frustrating Shit Creek breakdown and the pleasant days spent in Balsal seemed to have taken place months before, not just two weeks ago.

We reached Boca de Cupe by mid-afternoon, which was as far as Enrique could take me. I went in search of another boat to take me the rest of the way to Yaviza.

I was impatient to get to Yaviza and back on the Pan American Highway. I bargained as best I could with *Don* Antonio, the Panamanian storekeeper-consular official who had stamped the now-useless exit visa in my passport a month ago. He could arrange for his nephew Manuel and a helper to ferry Amigo and me to Yaviza in a larger piragua equipped with an outboard motor. But I was short of cash. Even though I had travelers checks, Antonio had a rule against accepting them. During our negotiations, however, he yielded and agreed to cash a check for me. Perhaps he had heard of my Noriega letter. More likely it was my wristwatch that I had tossed into the bargaining. We both knew that regardless of the amount he would receive when he converted the check, the watch would more than offset the larcenous one hundred dollar charge he set for the trip to Yaviza.

We quickly transferred Amigo and my gear from Enrique's piragua to the new boat. I settled up with Enrique and we said our farewells. Then I was off to Yaviza with Manuel. Even though the Tuira River meandered constantly, its deeper waters allowed us to go much faster and make better time than on the trip from Pucuru.

As we approached the point where the Chucunaque flows into the Tuira, the river broadened and we met a piragua carrying a passenger who asked to ride with us to Yaviza. Manuel maneuvered the piragua alongside the other to take on the neatly-dressed man. As he did, I objected vehemently.

"What the hell are you doing? Don't even think of getting into my piragua," I yelled at the man who was now standing up, ready to step into Manuel's canoe.

Everyone looked at me as if I had gone insane.

"It's too dangerous," I shouted angrily. "You'll capsize the piragua and dump my bike into the river. And who do you think is paying the outrageous price for this piragua ride anyway?"

Manuel calmly explained that the other passenger was the legislative representative for the area and that he had been summoned back to Panama City on official business. I should have known by now that in an area where rivers are the only reasonable means of transport, sharing piraguas was a common custom. Who was I, an outsider, to complain?

The man stepped easily between the piraguas, and I immediately felt ashamed for acting so irately. My dejection at having to retreat to Yaviza was getting to me, and I lapsed into an uncomfortable silence for the rest of the trip. I reminded myself that I would see these people again, that I would depend on their good will and help to get me through the Darien, because I resolved to return and succeed next year.

We arrived at Yaviza at dusk. In twelve hours I had completed a trip by river that had taken thirty-two days to travel by land. Manuel, the legislator and curious bystanders helped unload Amigo and push the bike up the muddy riverbank to the street. I reinstalled the tank and seat and tied my beat-up, dirt-encrusted equipment to the bike. I rode Amigo to the PDF headquarters, where I again received permission to sling my hammock in their *bohio*.

I shared the shelter with a young Japanese bicyclist who spoke English and Spanish so poorly I could not understand how he had gotten this far in his journey through the western hemisphere. Nor could I believe he was going to try to get through the Darien by himself. He knew so little of the obstacles he faced. Of course it would be easier for him with his light, ten-speed bicycle than it had been for me with Amigo. But he said he was short on money, had little knowledge of the area and expected to get through entirely on his own.

Over dinner and a couple of beers I tried to warn him of the formidable task he faced. But I could tell he did not understand. He responded only with a polite, al-most-perpetual Oriental smile that occasionally turned into a half-suppressed giggle.

That night, as I drifted in and out of a fitful slumber, I calculated all the possible hazards he would face. I never learned whether he made it through the Darien. And I still wonder about him, whether he succeeded, if he became a casualty of the rainy season or, perhaps, suffered the same fate as the Costa Rican on the mule.

I loaded Amigo early the next morning and guided the still-sputtering bike along Yaviza's deserted streets and headed for Panama City. Beyond Canglón I reached the wider, graveled surface of the Pan American High-way and was able to rev up the engine. With higher RPMs the motor smoothed out, and I geared up to speeds I had not reached for more than a month.

Late that afternoon I reached Panama City and headed out to Albrook Air Force Station in Balboa to put up at the Road Knights club. I spent the next few days working on Amigo, completely stripping and cleaning the bike to get rid of the layers of Darien mud. One club member, Matt Forslund, a talented young U.S. Air Force technician, easily traced the engine's misfiring to the bad spark plug wire which he then replaced.

I remained in Panama several weeks, recuperating and conducting a motorcycle safety course for the U.S. Air Force. The teaching was a welcome diversion which mollified the effects of my Darien defeat. The job also earned me a partial payback for the cost of the expedition — $1,217 that I had paid Loren Upton as my share of expenses, plus $180 and the watch for the piraguas back to Yaviza.

While in Panama I tracked down Bob Webb, who had made the Rokon motorcycle expeditions into the Darien in the early 1970s. Bob was still working for the Panama Canal Commission and lived at Fort Davis on the Atlantic side of the isthmus. I met him at the Mindi hobby shop where he modestly showed me the forty-four-foot sailboat, — the *Hunky Dory* — he was building "just to knock around on."

About forty years old, Bob was unpretentious — average in every way, so it seemed. Nothing in his demeanor revealed the determination and inner strength that drove him to challenge the Darien three times before succeeding. Bob said his first attempt in 1973 had started out as a light-hearted excursion, done without the large investment or elaborate support system employed by other expeditions. His Canadian-made Rokon cycle had a complex, low-geared, dual-drive system that powered both wheels. But the bike was a cranky beast prone to frequent failures which forced Bob to return home well short of his goal.

The next year he enlisted Ron Merrill, a friend, to accompany him. Both riding Rokons, they set out for the far side of the Darien. They made good progress at first,

Loren Upton (left) and me aboard a raft made from planks and two canoes take Amigo across the Chucunaque River at Yaviza.

Left. The 1985 "don't shoot him" letter signed by Gen. Noriega. *Below*. Amigo's license tag.

Above. Lawrence Upton guides the jeep "Discovery" onto a raft in the Chucunaque River at Yaviza. Pat Mercier, in cap, watches.

Left. Pat Mercier and Lawrence Upton rig Discovery for towing out of a ravine near Pinogana.

Above. Loren Upton directs *macheteros* in cutting through a log blocking the trail.
Below. Lawrence Upton, Pat Mercier and Loren Upton pause on the trail alongside Discovery and Amigo.

Discovery crossing the Tuira River near Pinogana.

Discovery anchored to a tree by
cables and ready for winching.

Amigo stuck in the muddy tracks
left by a bulldozer between
Pinogana and Boca de Cupe.

Above. Discovery, disabled in the Rio Eme valley, is tied off to a tree on the steep bank. A cable ties Amigo to the jeep. *Below.* Near Balsal, we use a raft to cross the Tuira River for the second time.

Above. Cuna Indians pose with me at the village of Pucuru. From left to right: Enrique, Manuel, Francisco Garrido. Francisco is the chief of the tribe at Pucuru.

Right. Daughter of the chief of the Choco Indians at Balsal astride Amigo.

Amigo and I used piraguas to go downriver from Pucuru to
Yaviza.

Above. Amigo and I about to depart for the Darien Gap in 1986.
Below. The entry on page 31 of my passport indicates I entered
Colombia through *"el Tapon del Darien"* — the Darien Gap.

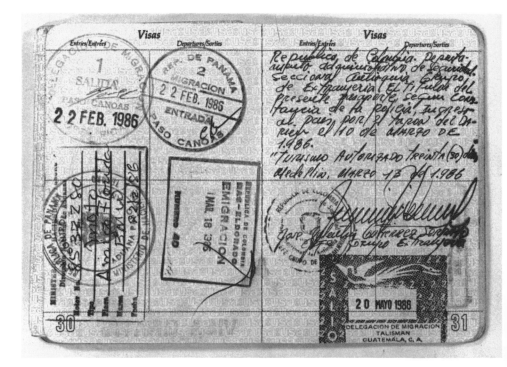

but the Rokons again proved to be cantankerous machines.

"We spent most of our time working on them rather than riding them," Bob said.

Despite their recurring mechanical problems they were able to penetrate the Darien to the vicinity of the Ipetí River, midway to the Colombian border, before they ran out of gas, food, good weather and time. They laid up the bikes in a lean-to and returned on foot to the Canal Zone, declaring a truce with the jungle until the next dry season.

More determined than ever, Bob and Ron retraced their route back to the Rokons early in 1975. They rehabilitated the motorcycles and set out again for the border. Relying heavily on help from the Indians along the way, they made it. After crossing into Colombia at Palo de las Letras, Bob admitted they "cheated a little" by loading the Rokons into piraguas and floating them down the Rio Cacarica to the Atrato River. There they transferred to a launch which took them to Turbo on the Caribbean. They shipped the bikes back to Colón, Panama, where they sold them and ended their careers as motorcycle adventurers.

"Would you do it again?" I asked.

"No, I really wouldn't want to. That kind of trip is a one-time deal. It was a fun thing that almost got out of hand. Now I'd rather get the boat finished and go roam around the Pacific."

I also talked later with Ron Merrill in Balboa. He confirmed much of what Bob had told me. Their story encouraged me, reassured me that it was possible to get a motorcycle through the gap and to the Atrato River.

But the trip I was planning differed from Bob and Ron's in ways that would make mine a more difficult trek. I would be going through alone, accompanied only by the guides I would hire. And I would have to wrestle a much heavier bike than the low, fat-wheeled Rokons. I would also not be bypassing the Atrato River's swamps by floating down the Atrato to Turbo as did most expeditioners. That was not the proposed route of the Pan American Highway. I was committed to following that dashed line the California biker had shown me in 1974. Somehow I would have to work my way through the swamps to Barranquillita to pick up the southern terminus of the main Pan American Highway. I wanted to stay as close as I could to the highway's proposed route, the route taken by the British expedition in 1971-72, and I intended to be as much a purist in the matter as was Major Blashford-Snell.

I left Panama cycling up the Pan Am through Costa Rica and running hard through Nicaragua, Honduras and El Salvador. In Guatemala I paused to present a motorcycle training program for Peace Corps personnel. From Guatemala I sped into Mexico. I was hurrying, not really letting the renewed pleasures of the road sink in. I was anxious to reach Florida and get home.

My thirty-three days in the Darien had strengthened the obsession. I was now caught up in the same kind of single-minded pursuit that would keep Loren Upton penned up in an open-sided jungle prison for the next nine months. But I had the freedom to act, to use Upton's tutelage to work out a strategy for the next campaign. I was going home defeated. I had lost the battle, but the war was still on. I swore with something approaching Upton's ardor that the next homecoming would be different — I would celebrate having closed the gap.

9

This Time Alone

Down to Gehenna or up to the Throne,
He travels the fastest who travels alone.

Rudyard Kipling
The Winners

At home I abandoned my regular activities, including my voluntary civic service. I banked the coals of the obsession by writing magazine stories of the expedition with Upton and presenting color slide shows. I also concentrated on motorcycle safety programs. It was a form of therapy — keeping me riding and flying out to the

Caribbean and back to Guatemala to give more Peace Corps training courses.

Between these sessions I prepared for my return to the Darien. I asked the U.S. representatives of BMW for help. They rewarded me with a special equipment package that transformed Amigo into an even closer replica of the BMW that had several times won the Paris-Dakar endurance run. The major item was a huge nine-gallon gas tank which made Amigo awkwardly top-heavy when filled. But the tank would be invaluable passing through both gas-starved Nicaragua and the Darien. I also received the best, most comfortable motorcycle seat ever made — a Denfeld police-style single saddle, behind which was a metal rail platform where I could strap my pack with elastic bungee cords.

BMW also suggested I have the original clutch plate replaced by a later, stronger unit to avoid the fatigue-induced failures that had happened on earlier models of the R80 G/S. Changing the clutch plate may not have been needed, but I thought of it as insurance against one type of breakdown that could leave me stranded who knows where.

In late 1985, as the time to return to the Darien drew near, my preparations focused on the details. I reopened my account with the automobile association for another Carnet. This time I had to post a seven-thousand-dollar bond. I also replaced the light jungle combat boots I had worn on the last trip with an expensive pair of snake-proof boots. They came with a guarantee of a replacement set to my heirs should the boots prove to be ineffective. I had not seen a single snake on last year's Darien expedition, but the odds were that I would eventually come into contact with one. In addition, the new boots gave me more ankle support which would help prevent another sprain.

Remembering the easily convertible economic value my watch had had in Boca de Cupe, I prevailed upon a jeweler friend, John Herbst, to obtain four cheap but expensive-looking analog wrist watches that I could use as barter. I concealed the watches, along with four thousand dollars in travelers checks, in a carefully created hiding place on the bike. In all the searches Amigo and I would undergo, the valuables were never discovered.

On February 12, 1986, I said goodbye again to my wife, mounted Amigo and rode away from home. I headed northwest out of Florida and around the Gulf Coast to Texas where I stopped for a brief meeting with my oldest daughter. Then I set out for Laredo to pick up the Pan American Highway at the International Bridge over the Rio Grande where the road had been ceremoniously inaugurated in 1936. I held a short ceremony of my own at the river, vowing to cover every mile of the main Pan American Highway to the south before returning to the United States.

Once across the Rio Grande I shook free of the 55 mph U.S. interstate speed limit and blasted past the heavy truck and bus traffic through Monterrey, San Luis Potosí and Querétaro to reach Mexico City in record time. From there I breezed down the now-familiar road to Oaxaca in Southern Mexico and on to Guatemala.

I rested a bit in Antigua, checking on the survival rates of my earlier Peace Corps motorcyclist trainees. I then rode quickly through El Salvador and Honduras. I sped through Nicaragua in only five hours, not having to worry about scrounging around for strictly rationed gasoline. Amigo's new tank took me all the way to Costa Rica with a gallon or two to spare.

As I crossed the border, friendly Costa Rican border guards told me of an English couple who had recently passed through riding a motorcycle with a sidecar. I shunned the delights of San Jose and hurried on to Panama to check in again at the Road Knights club.

I found several international visitors in residence at the club, including the English couple the Costa Rican border guards had told me about. Richard and Mopsa English were more than three years into an around-the-world cycle tour on a Triumph 650 Thunderbird with a Squire box sidecar. We had a delightful meeting and exchanged stories of our adventures.

I set about preparing for life in the jungle. Going it alone through the Darien gave me challenges I had not faced on last year's expedition. I visited the U.S. Army Tropic Test Center to beg a snake-bite kit and antidotes for killer bee stings. Doctor Chaniotis, a bearded, intensely animated entomologist, talked me out of taking snake bite anti-venin.

"Look, my adventurous friend. If you are bitten by a snake, you must be able to recognize the type of reptile and select the appropriate anti-venin. If you use the wrong antidote, you may well die from the effects of the remedy even before the venom takes effect."

He was persuasive and I consoled myself that I did have a pair of snake-proof boots. Dr. Chaniotis gave me a bee sting kit, and I added anti-malaria pills and water purification tablets to my supplies. I also renewed my shots for every tropical disease the medics thought I might be exposed to.

A fellow motorcycle safety instructor and Air Force pilot, Dick Garrett, had suggested I take along an emergency locater transmitter. Dick said aircraft carry the device which in the event of a crash automatically broadcasts a distress signal. Orbiting satellites pick up the coded beeps and retransmit them along with location data to international rescue centers. The transmitter appeared to be an ideal way for me to reach out from the jungle to call for help.

I contacted the U.S. Air Force search and rescue center at Howard Air Force Base. The officer in charge told me that an emergency locater transmitter could work for me, but I would have to acquire the device from commercial sources. He also said that because I would be in Panama, the air arm of the PDF rather than the U.S. Air Force would mount the rescue mission. I wondered just how much of an effort the Panamanians would put into rescuing a solo motorcyclist, even if he did have a kindly, year-old letter from their *comandante,* General Noriega.

Prowling around Paitilla Airport in Panama City I found that transmitters were available, but even a short-term rental would cost sixteen hundred dollars. I also learned that the transmitters activate automatically upon impact. With the falls Amigo and I would inevitably be taking on the jungle trails, I might not be able to keep the transmitter from sounding off inadvertently. Considering the drawbacks, I said the hell with it and decided to rely on Indian guides and, if necessary, the missionary communications network.

Another bit of well-meaning advice had to do with firearms. Ever since I began traveling in remote areas friends have encouraged me to carry a gun to defend myself. I've always believed, however, that a weapon, especially a handgun, would create more problems than it would ever solve. Just having a gun in my possession in some places could get me thrown in jail. And if I ever had to use it and was lucky enough to get in the first effective shot, the authorities would probably not treat me as a hero. After a lifetime of living with and using firearms, I had forsaken them. I did not need to defend myself so aggressively now. The Darien was not Korea or Vietnam. My survival in the jungle would depend on my own resources and on the help of Indians whom I could trust.

I budgeted one thousand dollars cash for the Darien passage, much of it in small-denomination bills. I knew I would have to buy my way through, and I didn't want to run short of money as I had last year.

I stripped Amigo down until just the seat, gas tank, engine, frame and wheels were still intact. This lightened the bike and offset the extra weight of the large-capacity gas tank. Even so, I could barely pick up the four hundred-pound bike when it fell over. I rigged a towing bridle capable of being used at the front and rear of the bike. I also packed yards of nylon tow ropes and two pulleys.

I stuffed my valuables, camera, extra lens and color slide film into the tank bag. I strapped my other gear, including a bulging backpack, to the seat's rear platform. Once into the jungles, though, to keep Amigo stripped down, I would have to have the Indians carry all the gear — my backpack, the tank bag, my hammock, ten days worth of trail rations and canned goods, water canteens and the extra five gallons of gas I intended to buy in Yaviza.

I planned to leave behind at the Road Knights everything not absolutely necessary to get Amigo and me through the Darien to Bogotá. I hoped to catch a hop on a U.S. military flight from Bogotá back to Howard Air Force Base in Panama, bringing with me the gear left over from the jungle passage. I would retrieve the equipment to restore Amigo to a highway-running configuration and fly back to Bogota. I would then start the South American phase of the journey.

Just before setting out, I contacted John Mercier, Pat's husband. He said that last year Pat had returned to Panama, and Loren Upton stayed in Pucuru with Discovery as he had pledged. He relieved his virtual imprisonment only by reading boxes of books that Pat shipped him through the missionaries. Upton's stay in Pucuru almost cost him his health. In August he had to be evacuated on the missionary plane to be treated for a severe case of dysentery.

But he returned to Pucuru a week later to wait out the rains. Pat and several of Upton's friends whom he had recruited for the trek had already joined him. The group had set out from Pucuru on January 14, right at the end of the rainy season, and was now on the trail to Paya. I would not be able to see them unless I hurried and followed their trail.

On March first I again set out for the Darien, heading east on the Pan Am on a loaded-down, awkwardly handling Amigo. I did not tarry but rode hard for

Yaviza. I found traffic on the dusty road much heavier than before, and I saw a quantum jump in the development of the previously isolated region. Even Yaviza was now blessed with regular bus service thanks to the road from Canglón being upgraded to an "all-weather" route.

Yaviza was quite hospitable to me. On this visit, my fourth, I was remembered — not just as the bearer of the Noriega letter, but as the man who wanted to challenge the Darien on his odd-looking motorcycle. Sergeant Morales was back, and he introduced me to his lieutenant who gave me the run of the PDF headquarters.

I quickly hired a piragua crew to take me to Boca de Cupe the next morning. Then I ran into a critical problem — there was no gasoline in Yaviza. The only fuel available was either diesel for the trucks and buses or premixed gas-oil for the outboard motors. Regular gasoline had been sold out and the resupply truck had not yet arrived. It was probably the broken-down tanker I had passed about a hundred miles west of Yaviza. But my boat crew assured me I could buy gasoline tomorrow at the depot in Pinogana.

At daybreak I was up and shaved and had Amigo packed by the time the nearby restaurant opened. I hungrily wolfed down a breakfast of beans and rice topped by a greasy fried egg. I did not know when I would again have an adequately cooked meal.

I waited on the riverbank for my two-man boat crew. But I grew anxious when the time we were to meet came and went without any sign of them. They showed up sheepishly two hours later — Darien time I thought. We loaded Amigo, minus the seat and gas tank, into the bottom of the piragua, wedging the bike in on its side. I loaded the other gear, being especially careful not to damage the fuel petcocks on the bottom of the tank. I then settled down on the detached motorcycle seat, readying myself for the trip back up the Chucunaque, Tuira and Pucuru rivers and the return to my contest with the Darien.

We passed the scar in the river's left bank that was our entry point into the jungle on last year's expedition. I was relieved not to have to retrace that route. I had already taken Amigo by land from Yaviza to Pucuru and had no desire to repeat the ordeal. My objective was to to get back to last year's stopping point in Pucuru by piragua, and push on from there through the rest of the Darien. The new route would be much harder than the route to Pucuru, and I needed to conserve my strength, supplies and resolve for the unknown regions ahead.

At Pinogana the boatmen and I visited the same store I had stopped at last year. But the proprietress said she had no gasoline, only the outboard pre-mix. But I thought differently. Last year she had sold regular gasoline to Upton, and I suspected that she had a separate drum of it somewhere.

We argued amiably, and she confessed that she did have gasoline. But her husband, who was off in the hills working his crops, had ordered her not to sell any of the precious fuel. I gently corrupted her by paying double the regular price for five gallons. From a rusty drum hidden behind the store the boatmen siphoned my reserve supply of gas into a plastic container.

We left Pinogana and wound our way up the twisting Tuira River to Boca de Cupe. I had to hire another boat to get me the rest of the way to Pucuru. But *Don* Antonio was not at his store, so I could not arrange for a piragua and had to stay overnight. I rented a room whose price included a plain but nourishing supper with my hosts. I thought the simple food and lumpy cot were comforts I would not encounter beyond Boca de Cupe.

The next morning I bargained with Antonio for another piragua and a two-man crew. After much haggling I agreed to pay sixty dollars to get Amigo and me to Pucuru. The Panamanians argued that the water level was so low they could not use the motor and would have to pole most of the way.

Indeed they did. It was slow going, especially after we turned away from the Tuira and started up the much smaller Pucuru River. The trip was a repeat of last year's return run with Enrique, and we all had to get out and push the piragua over the rocky, shallow streambed as we neared the village.

Just short of Pucuru we met another piragua going downstream loaded to the gunwales with bananas and sacks of rice, corn and beans. I recognized one of the boat's occupants as Francisco Garrido. We stopped our piraguas and greeted each other warmly. I gave him copies of pictures I had taken of him last year. He said he was going to Yaviza and would not return for a day or two. But he told me to contact Enrique about hiring guides to get me to Paya. The mid-river reunion ended all too quickly as we moved out on our separate courses.

At Pucuru we unloaded the motorcycle and my equipment with the excited help of most of the village's children, some of whom I remembered from last year. They eagerly helped me carry my gear to Francisco's house where I set up in the same room I had used before.

Regretfully, Enrique could not go with me to Paya. But he rounded up four young men who were eager to help. I rigged Amigo with the towing bridle and drilled them on how to pull the motorcycle using a heavy pulley anchored to a tree. Two would draw on the tow rope and the others would help me steady the bike or push from behind. The young men fell into the routine easily and enjoyed their roles, much to the envy of their friends. Not only had they been honored by being selected to go along on the expedition, but I had agreed to pay them six dollars each per day.

Now it was time for fun and games. I searched through my backpack and pulled out a frisbee, sending it sailing up the street for the youngsters to chase. I dug in the pack again and took out a hand air pump and inflating needle. Last year I had seen the children playing with an all-but-flat soccer and basketball because they lacked an inflating needle. The boys quickly located the nearly collapsed balls and we pumped them up. The youngsters, and a few adults, immediately began to kick up a cloud of dust around a basketball hoop and on a makeshift soccer field.

I called on the two American missionary couples who had been away on vacation during my stay in Pucuru last year. They were from the New Tribes Missions group of Sanford, Florida, just fifty miles from my home. They invited me to dinner, and we spent a pleasant evening discussing their work ministering to the Cunas and translating the Bible into the local dialect. The Mankins and Simmonses were modestly proud of their calling. I could not help but compare their motivation and dedication to that of the Central American and Caribbean Peace Corps workers to whom I had given motorcycle safety training.

But they were noticeably reticent to talk about Loren Upton. I noted a quick glance of concern between the missionaries when I asked about Upton's nine-month stay. They said only that Upton had moved the jeep to the outer edge of the village. With the aid of several villagers he built a shelter beside the jeep and passed the time by reading. He spent little time in the village and had only infrequent contact with the missionaries.

I sensed there was more to tell, but my hosts let the conversation taper off. I thanked them for their hospitality and bid them farewell in the deepening dusk. What they had seemingly left unsaid troubled me. And I was disturbed again the next day when I asked one of my Indian guides about Upton.

The young Cuna shrugged his shoulders noncommittally and said only that Upton was, *"un hombre muy violento."* I surmised that the isolation may have sharpened Upton's quick temper and provoked him into some sort of confrontation with the villagers.

Thinking about Loren Upton kept me from sinking into an easy sleep. I knew if I could not catch up with him and his expedition, I might never be able to find out from him just what he had endured during his nine-month stay in the village. I was also filled with anticipation for the next day's trek which would take me past last year's stopping point. I tossed for what seemed hours on the floor of the sleeping room before drifting off into a sleep that lasted until daybreak.

10

Hard on Upton's Trail

Take calculated risks.
That is quite different from being rash.

General George S. Patton, Jr.
Letter to Cadet George S. Patton, IV

On my expedition's fourth day, Francisco's wife, wrinkled and gnarled far beyond her husband's apparent age, laid out a breakfast of fried plantains, beans, rice and incredibly strong coffee — good fare for the day ahead. My youthful, spirited crew was up early also, and we split up the equipment between the young men. One would carry the tank bag, another the backpack and the third would tote the five-gallon gas container. The fourth man would handle my jungle hammock and the extra water jugs.

We set out with me in the lead, riding Amigo confidently down to the river's edge, escorted by an excited gaggle of children and many of the older villagers. I easily forded the Pucuru, now less than axle deep and bounced up the shallow bank onto the path that Francisco and I had covered on foot last year.

The ride started out as a fun run for me. I stood up on Amigo's foot pegs and easily bumped over the small rocks and tree roots along the trail leading uphill beside the river. I dared not look sideways down the fearsome escarpment. I could see signs where the path had been widened to accommodate Upton's jeep which had passed this way some six weeks before.

According to the Indians, Upton had paid the residents of Pucuru a handsome bonus to start their annual path clearing in December, a month early and before the rains had abated. As soon as the trail had been cleared, he, Pat Mercier and the others had set out with the jeep for Paya. They were leaving me with the same kind of clearly defined, easily negotiable trail that the AMC expedition had provided for Upton in 1979. Unkindly, I could not help but wonder if Upton would bill me retroactively for a share of the cost of the work.

Although I was following Upton's trail and religiously applying the experience I had picked up from him last year, I still could not ride Amigo very far before having to halt at some impassable barrier and wait for the Indians to catch up. Even in the few weeks since

Upton's passage, more trees had fallen across the path, and we had to attack each one of the frustrating blockades.

The quickest tactic was to ride around the downed tree, roaring off into the heavy undergrowth in a Patton-like flanking movement while urging Amigo to power through the tangled vines and matted brush. Although the maneuver was fast, it was also reckless. Among the jungle's vegetation were vicious black palm fronds that carried barbed needles which could only be removed from human skin by surgery. If left, they festered and became infected. One of our trail guides last year got a broken-off barb impaled in his leg. He had to hobble back to the dispensary at La Palma to have the ugly spine cut out. Should I hit or fall on a black palm frond, it could very well mean the end of my Darien quest.

So we developed several alternative tactics to overcome the downed trees. On occasion we would bodily lift Amigo over a reclining log. Sometimes we would build up ramps of branches on each side of the fallen tree so I could ride the bike up and over it. Several times we laid the bike over on its side and slid it underneath the tree. But the loss of precious gasoline that would leak from the carburetors and the gas tank's air vent made me nervous. Only as a last resort did I ask the Indians to hack through tree trunks with their machetes so we could drag the separated section aside enough to let me slip through. The Upton technique just took too long.

The straight-line distance to Paya is about twelve miles, an easy half-day walk for the Indians. But our frequent trail-clearing stops, which were becoming more welcome to me as rest periods, meant we would not

reach Paya before dark. So I decided to camp just beyond the junction of the Pucuru and Tupalisa rivers.
Two of the Indians stayed with me. I allowed the other
two to return to Pucuru after they promised to report
back at dawn.

Our first camp by the riverside was idyllic, with
clear, cool water to wash in and to use for shaving. This
was a daily routine which I refused to disrupt, even at
the worst of times. Keeping a reasonably neat appearance would set me apart from many of the scruffy travelers I had seen on the trail.

Maintaining personal hygiene also had a practical
value. Bathing daily allowed me to avoid the crotch and
feet infections so common in the jungle. And by stripping down I could go after the *bichos,* a most descriptive-
sounding name for the ticks, chiggers and other vermin
that had hopped on me and my clothing as I thrashed
around in the brush. If left on, the ticks buried into the
skin to feed on blood. They were almost impossible to dig
out without leaving the head under the skin where it
would ulcerate and become infected.

I also took preventive measures by smearing myself
with the Army's potent bug repellant. Squeezing the lotion from little olive drab plastic bottles, I would apply it
liberally to my skin as well as my socks and boot tops. I
also spread it on my jeans — the legs, crotch, fly zipper
and waistband. The lotion was a powerful formula of
DEET, and it was so effective I believe it must surely
cause latent damage to humans. No remedy can be that
good without having a malignant payback somewhere
down the line.

I brought out my small, one-burner gas camp stove

and heated water to add to the plastic pouches of dried trail rations. They made a tasty and nutritious meal but were not very filling. But at least I had variety, far more so than the steady diet of beans and rice of last year's expedition where the only change was the order in which the two staples were served. The two Indians had brought along small packets of plantains and rice wrapped in leaves.

Breakfast, after a tranquil night, was a pleasant repast, and I shared my powdered coffee with the two young Indians. They had leftovers from their supper for breakfast, licking the leaves hungrily to devour the last grains of rice. As soon as the two village overnighters arrived we moved out along the portion of the trail that was the responsibility of the Paya tribe. With civic chauvinism my guides pointed out that the Paya trail cutters had been much less conscientious and we had to work around and through far more barriers than on the day before.

But the terrain also contributed to making the passage more difficult. Nearing Paya the hills became progressively more frequent and steeper. I could see many signs of Upton's passage — hacked down vegetation decaying along the trail and gouges in trees from tow cables and pulleys. The Indians said Upton had taken five days to get the jeep to Paya. He averaged a little more than a mile and a half per day, about the same pace as last year.

Paya sits on the crest of a U-shaped ridge formed by a bend in the Rio Paya. Formerly the capital of all the Cuna tribes, Paya was once the center of a glorious empire that reportedly numbered a million subjects. Those days are long lost to antiquity I thought as I bumped down the washboard-like red dirt path into the village that now appeared to house only a hundred or so Indians.

When my guides caught up with me they directed me to the corregidor's house at the far end of the village. With their task completed, I paid off my young helpers and gave each a warm *abrazo,* or hug, and wished them well on their return to Pucuru.

The village chief showed me where to park Amigo and to sling my hammock. I told him I would need a six-man replacement crew to help on the trail to Colombia. He promised to arrange for a team by evening. I scouted around Paya but found little of interest, so I decided to return to my camp and take a short siesta.

I awoke with a start. Heavy drops of water were pelting and penetrating my jungle hammock's cover. Rain! It's supposed to be the dry season. Any substantial rainfall would turn the trails to mud and make riding Amigo virtually impossible. Mercifully, the shower was short. But I hoped it was not an omen of an early rainy season.

The missionaries in Pucuru had told me another New Tribes member was also working in Paya, and I set out to pay him a visit. I saw him but never did meet him. The missionary was standing on the high bank across the Paya River from the village. He waved to me as a single-engine plane, a New Tribes Missions resupply flight, banked to land on a rough, dirt airstrip.

I was just about to run down to the river and cross over to the airstrip when two PDF soldiers in camouflage uniforms carrying FN rifles approached me. They requested that I accompany them to their headquarters about a half mile from the village. It was not a demand, but a polite invitation issued in the name of their commander, Lieutenant Miranda. I did not feel threatened. A report on me and my Noriega letter had probably been signalled ahead. This visit would be a courtesy call.

We walked upriver along a well-maintained path laid out with obvious military precision and bordered by whitewashed marking stones. The path ended at the river, and the soldiers poled me across in a small piragua. We disembarked at the entrance to a barbed-wire-enclosed PDF compound. Lieutenant Miranda, a young, impeccably uniformed officer, was there to meet me.

The lieutenant invited me to join him for supper in the open, thatched-roof dining hall. The meal was a surprise — a tender, juicy venison steak from wild jungle deer and American-style baked beans. I complimented him on the menu. He smiled and said it was one of the compensating perks that offset the isolation and career obscurity of his year-long assignment at Paya.

Lieutenant Miranda was commander of the easternmost outpost of the PDF, a modest garrison charged with protecting the most vulnerable flank of the republic. Among his duties was immigration control. He said non-Panamanians constantly entered the country through the Darien. Many were without documents, and a fair share were dangerous criminals. But he said his primary mission was to interdict the flow of drugs coming through the Darien from the cocaine processing laboratories in Colombia. His troops patrolled the jungles trying to intercept the "mules" — the heavily laden, human drug transporters.

He cautioned me to be alert for the *drogistas*. They automatically assumed any foreigner, especially an American, was an agent or informant of the Drug Enforcement Administration. And they would kill without question. He also warned me about gold miners and grave robbers who would react violently to intruders who they felt threatened their illegal activities.

I asked Lieutenant Miranda about the Upton expedition, but he had been on leave when the jeep and its crew came through the area. He said he knew only that the group had spent little time in Paya before pressing on toward the border at Palo de las Letras and were now somewhere in Colombia.

Dusk was approaching when I said goodbye to Lieutenant Miranda and left the PDF headquarters. I had enjoyed the visit and was much impressed with the lieutenant. I would have liked to learn more about his background and how he had acquired his impressive military bearing, which was far above that of the typical PDF officer. I also wanted to pry deeper to find out his feelings toward his commander, General Noriega. But the timing was not right for this sort of exchange, so I regretfully let it lie.

The two soldiers poled me back across the river in the piragua, but I declined their offer to keep me company on the way back to Paya. As I walked slowly along the deserted trail, I savored the early evening silence and thought about the dinner-table discussion and the prospects for the rest of the journey through the Darien.

Back in Paya I met again with the chief. He had no sympathetic, personal interest in my venture as had Francisco Garrido of Pucuru. This chief looked upon my request for help strictly as a business proposition and a way to insure my quick departure from his village. He said he had selected six young men to help me through to Colombia and their pay would be eight dollars per day per man.

I protested that this was far more than I had paid before for guides. I thought for a moment about doing my own hiring. If I bypassed the chief, who undoubtedly received a kick-back from his recruits, I could probably cut the cost. But I reminded myself that the reliability and loyalty of men assigned the job by their chief was at least partially guaranteed. If anything should happen to me, the guides and the chief would share the responsibility. I needed that kind of security to help offset the dangers Lieutenant Miranda had warned me about.

I bargained with the chief to a point where we agreed I would pay the daily rate but the Indians would provide their own food. They would stay with me as long as I needed them. But the chief reminded me that we would enter into a different tribal region on the Colombian side of the border, and the Cunas would not want to stay for long outside their own boundaries.

We did not make an auspicious start the next morning. I awoke early and crawled out of the hammock to gulp down a quick, cold breakfast of right-out-of-the-can chicken. I repacked my gear and readied Amigo for the trail. My crew — six boisterous young men in their late teens and early twenties — gathered excitedly around the motorcycle. They pawed through my equipment, foiling my attempts to have them practice the rigging-and-towing routine.

I gave up on the idea and sent the Indians to scour

the village for food — beans, rice, fruit and canned goods. The search was disappointing, little food was available. Even my offer of ridiculously high prices produced only a large sack of rice, a bag of beans, and several rusty cans of fruit cocktail and spam-like meat which was imported from such geographically implausible places as Denmark and Argentina.

I figured Upton's expedition had cleaned out the cupboards and the villagers had not yet had a chance to restock. I was concerned. Once on the trail I saw little chance of resupply. The short rations meant that we could stand no delays on the route ahead or we would run out of food.

I impatiently waved the crew onward to the other end of the village and the riverbank. I could clearly see the skidding path left by Upton's jeep where it had maneuvered in four-wheel drive down a steep slope to the water. My crew, and about half the village, watched as I hooked up the bridle to Amigo's rear frame. I instructed the six Indians how to pay out the tow rope as I braced myself alongside the bike, guiding it down the bank.

I could just barely keep Amigo upright as the motorcycle splashed into the shallow, rock-filled Paya River. I didn't bother riding Amigo across, but reversed the tow rope and had the Indians pull the bike to the other side. The far bank turned out to be lower but much steeper, and we were confronted with our first major task. There was no way I could ride up the bank, and there were no trees around to which I could anchor a pulley. Finally I enlisted the help of several of the onlookers, and we bodily lifted Amigo up to the beginning of a narrow path into the heavy underbrush.

I could not believe that Upton had taken his jeep out of the river at this point. With no trees available he could not have winched the jeep up the bank. Then one of the Indians said that Upton had driven upstream to a lower point on the bank behind which were trees he could use as anchors.

I had just learned two lessons — I needed more guidance from my guides, and I would need more help on the trail. So I sent one of the Indians, Mauricio, back to the village to ask the chief to send two more men to bolster the team. Although the added cost concerned me, time was beginning to weigh even more heavily on my mind. I simply could not afford any delays.

Upton's trail was visually easy to follow, but the debris left by his, and now my, *macheteros* caused the same problems as last year. The slick, round bamboo stalks and slippery palm and plantain fronds made Amigo's tires repeatedly slide out. The trail turned into a sporty course where staying upright was sometimes impossible, and Amigo and I routinely fell over. Sometimes, though, the going would be easier where I could pick my own path, straightening out the curves Upton had to take to keep his jeep on more level ground.

The further we got from Paya the worse the trail became. The rough path now ran along hogback ridges with steep drop-offs on each side. In places, the trail had narrowed to no more than shoulder width, despite the work Upton's crew had done to get the jeep through. We encountered frequent obstacles that put the crew and myself to sweating, grunting work with our hands, machetes, ropes and the pulley.

This section of the trail also posed a particular danger for me riding the motorcycle. I had to watch closely for huge ceiba trees whose roots ran along the surface of the thin-soiled rain forest. The blade-like roots created channels that would catch and deflect Amigo's front tire toward the tree.

Once, as I was picking my way along a narrow ridge, Amigo's front tire caught on a root. The handlebars were almost wrenched from my hands, and the bike lurched uncontrollably toward the thick base of the tree. Amigo slammed into the trunk and the impact threw me off. The bike caromed off the tree, barely missing me, and catapulted down a slope, sliding through deep underbrush with wheels in the air and engine still running.

As Amigo slid upside down, the handlebar throttle rolled itself wide open and the bike's rear wheel rotated wildly. I scrambled after the bike, watching gasoline gush from the inverted carburetors and fearing a blazing explosion at any moment. I reached Amigo and grabbed for the emergency cut-off switch to shut the engine down. I turned the fuel valve off and tried to get Amigo upright. On the steep incline I was only able to get Amigo onto its side, and the bike slid further down the slope.

When the Indians caught up with me, we hooked up the rope and pulley and hauled Amigo back to the crest of the ridge. I looked over the bike. Amazingly, it appeared practically undamaged. And when I turned the ignition on, Amigo stammered and coughed to life. But later I would find that the front fork triple clamp and brace had been bent and the front brake master cylinder would begin to leak.

We made several more miles that day before coming

upon a small clearing that appeared to be used by travelers as a camp site. I decided to call a halt and camp for the night. I took time to get acquainted with the two new guides Mauricio had gone back to Paya to get this morning. One was Alonso, a man about thirty years old. His relative maturity made him seem reticent compared to the six original, sometimes-rowdy crew members. Surprisingly, Alonso had brought along his eleven-year-old son as the eighth member of the crew.

What a mix we have now I thought. My first inclination was to send father and son back to Paya. But then I figured that perhaps Alonso would lend some adult leadership to the restive young men.

As for Alonso's son, I decided to assign him the job of water boy and nicknamed him Gunga Din. But that bit of whimsy created a problem explaining to the Indians the significance of the name. I had never before tried to translate Kipling's poetry into Spanish. I just draped the canteens and water bottles around the boy's neck and told him that whenever I called for water, I expected him to come running. The youngster broke into a broad grin of agreement, and we began an arrangement that was to work out well for all of us, at least most of the time.

Four of the Indians asked if they could go back to Paya for the night. I agreed on the condition that they return at daybreak. At least their departure for the night would save some precious food. As they left, the others started a fire to cook their beans and rice. They also gathered leaves and palm fronds over which they spread plastic ponchos to serve as beds.

After I fixed my meal the tropical sun faded rapidly

and the darkness sent me to my jungle hammock. I was comfortably tired, and quite satisfied that I had paced myself well. I listened to the low murmur of the Indians talking in their own dialect and tried to sort out the various jungle sounds before sinking into a placid sleep.

When the sun came up it brought the seventh day of my expedition. The day on the trail went well and by mid-afternoon we were nearing the end of our trek from Paya to the Palo de las Letras monument that marked the Panamanian-Colombian border.

Less than a mile from the border we came upon the red hulk of a rear-engine Corvair automobile. The abandoned car marked the spot where twenty-five years ago the General Motors Corvair convoy expedition had come to an end. Three of the cars accompanied by three four-wheel drive trucks set out to cross the Darien from Panama to Colombia. The expedition struggled for months to reach the border. As they penetrated deeper into the Darien the Corvairs could not even be driven and had to be towed in stages by the trucks. Finally, the expedition's leader called it quits and had two of the Corvairs towed back. He left the third sitting at the spot we were now at.

The brush had recently been removed from around the Corvair, which lay on the side of a ridge. The Indians said Upton's men had cleared it so that Pat Mercier could photograph the car. The Corvair had long ago been stripped of its useful parts, except for a heavy towing chain which was still wrapped around its front bumper. Disregarding a scattering of rust spots, the four-door sedan was in surprisingly good condition for having been abandoned in the jungle for a quarter of a century.

I took my own photographs and the young men frolicked in and around the car. I hoped they would not encounter a deadly coral snake and huge spider nesting inside as had Major Blashford-Snell's British expeditioners. Then we moved out. We worked our way along the ridges covering the last mile to the border and reached the hilltop clearing — Palo de las Letras — that marked the frontier. The site was named for an old, lightning-scarred tree with carved inscriptions. But in the late 1930s a crude cement and stone marker replaced the tree. Inscribed on its base was a misspelled indication that this was the "Colmbia" border.

I ordered a stop for the day. We set up camp at the marker, which served the Indians and myself as a make-shift table. After we cooked our meals, we lolled about enjoying the tranquil setting. I took several photos of the monument and a nearby helicopter landing pad, marked by a rough "H" made of logs. Then I sat down to record the day's events in my journal.

Suddenly the Indians called to me and pointed to the sky. Two beautifully colored birds were gliding elegantly over the ridge. Their widespread wings and extended tails displayed an array of bright, rainbow-hued feathers. The Indians were gesturing and chattering excitedly. They explained that the birds were very rare and seldom seen in this area. I guessed that they were quetzales, which are sacred to Indians throughout Central America. Most people see the birds only in the engravings on the currency of Guatemala, which is called the quetzal.

I watched intently as the birds swooped to a graceful landing on a branch of a dead tree and began a series of intricate movements. I thought it must be a mating dance. The Cunas tried to explain the pirouetting and bobbing of heads, but their rudimentary Spanish was not equal to the delicate movements of the birds. Suddenly it was over and the birds launched themselves into flight, coming back overhead in close formation. The two birds made a wondrous display which left all of us in reverential silence.

I settled down again to continue my writing but lapsed instead into deep rumination over the day's events. When I stirred from my reverie, I realized the Indians were also quiet. Eusebio, their self-appointed spokesman, was looking at me and asked what I was thinking.

"*Pues, es muy difícil* — It's very hard for me to explain," I stammered. "The sight of the birds seemed like a reward of some kind."

"A reward? For what?" Eusebio asked.

"Because...by reaching Palo de las Letras I have become the first motorcyclist to have travelled from one end of the Republic of Panama to the other. And I am very grateful to be here."

I did not expect that Eusebio and the other Indians would grasp the geographic enormity of the feat, but they surprised me. They jumped to their feet and began clapping and cheering. My emotions welled up inside me, and I felt a great affection for these young men. They had guided me and helped me get here. I had entrusted my survival to them, and they had proven to be worthy protectors. Thanks to them and the Cuna Indians from Pucuru, I had achieved part of my goal.

My feelings and fatigue from the heavy work of the

day drove me to my hammock in the deepening twilight, and I quickly fell into a contented sleep — the last I would enjoy while still in the Darien.

11

Trouble Across the Border

'I 'ope you liked your drink,' sez Gunga Din.

Rudyard Kipling
Gunga Din

Despite the bright sunlight cascading into the hilltop clearing, the Indians were slow to rouse themselves. They seemed almost reluctant to leave this peaceful campsite and cross over into Colombia. It had nothing to do with the border itself. Political boundaries meant nothing to them. They were exempt from the ordinary

Panamanian and Colombian immigration rules and could pass freely between the two countries. These Indians were bound by far more ancient customs than an arbitrary line drawn between two republics.

We would soon be entering the Los Katíos national park region — a different tribal territory. Despite the ethnic similarities between the Cunas and the Katíos, my crew did not want to discuss the Colombian tribe. Even Osvaldo, normally the most obliging of the Indians, simply shrugged and turned away when I asked him about the Katíos.

The Indians dawdled while collecting their meager belongings, and I tinkered with the motorcycle. Finally we got underway, straggling out onto the path leading east, back into the jungle. I fired up Amigo and slowly moved ahead, carefully watching for signs of Upton's jeep — slashed underbrush, the occasional cut-into-sections downed tree or cable cuts in trees.

I almost missed it, but the trail took an abrupt turn to the right. I angled sharply to follow Upton's trail, but the Indians called out, pointing me back to the east. Then I realized that Upton had turned south, going parallel to the border to avoid entering the park. Apparently, he did not plan to test the Los Katíos vehicle ban. He was skirting the park and moving toward the Rio Peranchito.

For a moment I debated following Upton's trail and perhaps finding the comfort of fellow expeditioners, but I quickly abandoned the impulse. I did not find appealing the idea of again subordinating myself to Upton's domineering control and limiting my speed to the grinding crawl of the tow cable wrapping around the roller of the jeep's winch. Even if I caught up with Upton, I knew the terrain to the south was infernally bad. Upton himself dreaded the desolate area that was so abominable even the Pan American Highway surveyors had rejected it as a possible route. The engineers and politicians instead had settled on a route further east which sliced through Los Katíos. And I was committed to this route, even though conservationists had since imposed the ban on vehicular travel through the park. I hoped Amigo, being a motorcycle, would be less offensive to the park officials than Upton's jeep and his larger entourage. And I also assumed that my Noriega letter would guarantee me professional courtesies.

Simple logistics also dictated that I go straight ahead. My stock of canned food and packets of trail rations was dwindling rapidly. And the Indians' burlap sacks of rice and beans were nearly empty. Even more serious, I had used the last of my reserve supply of gasoline to top off Amigo's tank. No, I had to stick to my original plan of allowing only two weeks at the most to reach Barranquillita, thirty miles beyond the Atrato River. Any delays would force me to abandon Amigo to the jungle, like the Corvair and the Rokons, and break out of the Darien on foot.

The Indians were now anxious to get me moving, so I set my course to the east, heading into Los Katíos. I would make for the Colombian park ranger station at Cristales. But as soon as I turned away from the jeep's trail the going became infinitely harder. We no longer had even a footpath to follow, and the *machetero* crew had to work strenuously to cut through the increasingly thick vegetation.

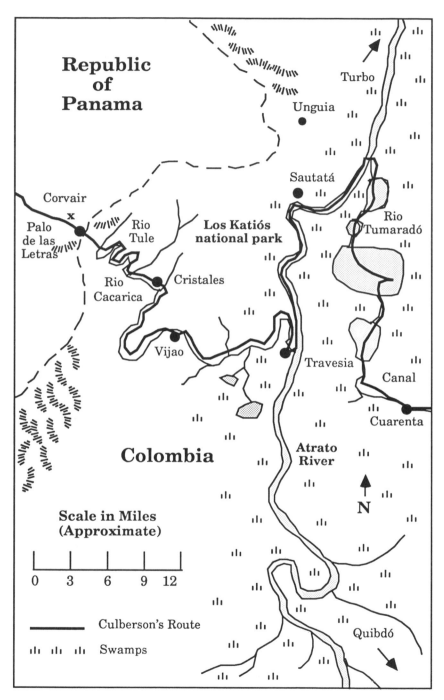

**Republic
of
Panama**

Turbo

Unguia

Sautatá

Corvair

x

Palo
de las
Letras

Rio
Tule

**Los Katiós
national park**

Rio
Tumaradó

Rio
Cacarica

Cristales

Vijao

Travesia

Canal

Cuarenta

Colombia

**Atrato
River**

N

**Scale in Miles
(Approximate)**

0	3	6	9	12

——— Culberson's Route

ılı ılı ılı Swamps

Quibdó

Darien Gap Area — Colombia

Our route now was an abrupt change from the almost park-like trails we had moved along on the Panamanian side of the border. We were now trending downward from the crests of the ridges, heading for the marshy lowlands and reeking swamps of the Atrato River basin.

The undergrowth quickly changed from the fairly thin upland rain forest vegetation to the distinctly thicker, more disorganized ground cover of a tropical jungle. Only by cutting our way through with the machetes could we make any headway. The air was still, and the atmosphere became fetid as the temperature and humidity rose to almost unbearable levels.

Both the Indians and I had to stop repeatedly to rest and take great gulps of water which quickly emptied our containers. Young Gunga Din was hard put to keep us resupplied. To fill our water containers we found only occasional trickling rivulets and stagnant, scum-covered pools left over from the rainy season.

Gunga Din returned from one replenishment mission and proudly passed the canteens around. Before any of us could take our first swallow, Eusebio pointed to the clear plastic two-quart jug I was holding and began laughing. I looked closer and saw debris, flies, mosquitoes and even small leeches milling about in the murky water.

I nearly gagged at the thought of almost having drank from the jug. I rigged a strainer using a clean handkerchief and managed to trap most of the visible solid trash and still-wriggling organisms as I poured between canteens. I dumped a mega-dose of halazone and iodine water purification tablets into the containers. But the Indians refused to share the now even viler-smelling water. Having spent their lives in the area, maybe their internal workings were naturally resistant to untreated water, even water as bad as this. But I was damned if I was going to risk getting sick in the jungle. Better to barf from an overdose of iodine than have leeches work on my insides like they did on the outside of the skin.

The water crisis ended when we reached the Rio Tule. This was the first stream beyond the border, and the waters now flowed into the Caribbean rather than the Pacific. Although more creek than river, the Tule had steep banks cut by the rainy season's raging torrents. The Indians said we would have to cross the winding Tule five or six more times before reaching the larger Rio Cacarica, which would be my outlet to the Atrato from the Los Katíos region. What the Indians said confirmed the excellent description and hand-drawn maps in my *Backpackers Guide,* a paperback published by Bradt Enterprises. I found the book to be far more reliable than the official maps of the area.

We hooked the tow rope to the rear of the motorcycle and slowly lowered it to the rocky stream bed. We crossed the Tule and found the opposite bank to be a near-vertical wall about ten feet high. This was going to be our toughest crossing so far. The sheer bank did not allow a straight draw to a pulley anchored to a tree, which had worked well on gentler slopes. And the steep angle and precarious footing prevented me from using Amigo's engine to help get the cycle up and over the bank. So we resorted to dragging and bodily lifting Amigo up the embankment.

Once we had Amigo out of the river bed, we resumed

the slow hacking of a trail through the jungle. But we had gone only a few hundred yards when we again came upon on another steep bank of the serpentine Tule. Tired, thirsty, hungry and frustrated, I could not see the obvious. I had forgotten the lesson learned in crossing the Paya River, but Eusebio impatiently remembered.

"Why not just ride the motorcycle down the river-bed?" he asked. "That way we can avoid all the rest of the crossings."

I was taken aback by the simplicity and logic of his idea. Even though riding Amigo along the muddy, rock-strewn streambed seemed formidable, it would be less strenuous than the repetitive crossings. I gave Eusebio an *abrazo* of thanks and organized the crew into action.

We lowered Amigo down the bank, and I mounted up. I edged out into the shallow stream, trying to dodge the moss-covered rocks and bumping over slab-like bed-rock outcroppings. The Indians served as outriggers, helping me balance Amigo and pulling me through frequent bog-downs in mud and sand.

Our pace was moderate but satisfying. We stopped only once — to clear the way of a six-foot snake of indeterminate species which we surprised at the water's edge. I took several photographs of the wary reptile, and then the younger Indians threw rocks at it. The snake fled up the bank and into the bush with an astonishing burst of frantic, wiggling motion.

This was the first snake I had seen in all those weeks of jungle travel. Osvaldo said it was harmless. He claimed that the most poisonous snakes were the most aggressive. This snake was neither, but Osvaldo still shook his head in loathing.

By mid-afternoon we had splashed and stumbled for several miles along the Tule, but I calculated our straight-line progress as only about a mile. Rounding one of the river's meanders, the Indians guided me to a depression in the bank. We heaved Amigo up and onto a faint path.

"This is the route to the Cacarica River," Eusebio said. "We have only a little farther to go."

I was not reassured. The jungle was thicker than ever, and the terrain was broken into small, angular hills. We began a maddeningly slow routine of continuously chopping and slicing to clear the path and then rigging Amigo for towing up the hills and sometimes even down the precipitous slopes.

At one point the Indians cleared the trail along a stretch of gently sloping ground, and I rode the bike slowly across the slope. But Amigo's wheels ran over some slick sap-filled cuttings left by the trail breakers. Amigo slid out from under me, and I fell off the bike on the downhill side. Amigo came right after me, landing on the back side of my left thigh and pinning me under the muffler's hot tail pipe. I screamed in agony as the metal burned through my jeans. The Indians ran to lift the bike off me. In his haste to help me, Eusebio grabbed the exhaust and suffered a painful burn on his palm.

When we all calmed down, I decided we had had enough expeditioning for the day, and we set up camp on the spot. I broke out my medical kit with its modest supplies and ministered as best I could to my thigh and Eusebio's hand with burn cream, gauze pads and adhesive tape.

With their hard labor and the hearty appetites of

youth, the Indians had already run out of the food they had brought from Paya and had to forage in the jungle. Several of them set about cutting wood and starting a fire while the others took off in search of plantains, nuts, roots and wild sugar cane. When they returned, they sliced and boiled the plantains and bolted down the pasty, tasteless lumps. I opened a can of tuna fish and added it to a broth I made from one of my few remaining packets of trail rations.

I idly considered developing and patenting "The Darien Gap Guaranteed Weight-Loss Program." My meager diet, continual exertion and barely offset loss of body fluids through constant sweating had already made me take up two notches in my belt. In all, the Darien would rob me of twenty pounds.

At dusk I strung up my hammock and climbed into the swaying, coffin-like cocoon. Although I was completely exhausted, I tossed restlessly, still hurting from the muffler burn. I knew I had stressed my fifty-six-year-old body past all reasonable limits.

My deep-down weariness seriously concerned me. This kind of fatigue led to mistakes in judgement that could mean disaster here in the wilds. In my condition I could easily inflict an incapacitating injury or an unstoppable bleeding wound. Far from timely medical aid or evacuation, such a trauma could very well take my life. I resolved not to ride Amigo in the jungle and to use the engine only when needed to reinforce the rope and pulley on the uphill climbs.

I was now reduced to what British writer Miles Clark called "the utterly unglamorous business of survival, of simply not dying." Death, according to Clark, would be nature's way of telling me my expedition wasn't going as well as it should.

I tried to find a more comfortable position in the hammock. But as if to underscore my mental and physical condition, the hammock fought back and threw me to the ground, ripping the mosquito netting. Cursing, I climbed back inside and faded in and out of a fitful sleep.

I awoke groggily during the night to the sound of the Indians stirring about. Eusebio, as usual, was the noisiest. He came over to the hammock and asked to borrow my flashlight. I refused angrily, telling him and the others to be quiet and let me sleep. In my semi-stupor I could not understand why they were still up. But I was too tired to worry about it.

I awoke well before dawn, sore and still weary almost beyond care. I lay in my hammock until first light and then crawled out. Eusebio emerged excitedly from his makeshift poncho bedroll.

"Señor Edwin, we have a plan for you to get down the river to Vijao, the first village in Colombia."

Not knowing what the hell he was talking about, I stared at him blankly.

"There are two Colombians waiting for you at the river, to take you and the motorcycle down the Cacarica to the village on the other side of Los Katíos."

Still sluggish and confused, I questioned how could this be.

"They are making a raft for the motorcycle, and they also have a piragua. All we have to do is meet them at the river."

Then I realized what had caused last night's commotion. Eusebio and several other Indians had taken off in the night — without my flashlight — and gone to the river to make a deal with some boatmen. But, I wondered, how did the Indians know the boatmen were there? Was it by chance, or were they that familiar with the area? Or was the Darien jungle telegraph at work again?

The questions intrigued me, but I could not fault Eusebio's initiative. Although our agreement was open-ended, the Indians were anxious to return to Paya. I was grateful that they had stayed with me this far into Colombia. I was even happier that they had arranged a hand-off to get me through the next part of my journey.

We quickly broke camp without eating and the Cunas started chopping away at the vegetation. Eusebio and Mauricio helped me wheel Amigo along the hacked-out trail. We had less than a mile of jungle to traverse to reach the Cacarica River, but never had we struggled so hard. Climbing the last hill before the river, we managed to break my industrial-strength pulley. We had to substitute the smaller pulley and reinforce it with sheer muscle power to drag Amigo to the low crest overlooking the Cacarica.

Two Colombians were waiting for us on the bank. Garrapata — "the tick" — was a short, grizzled man who proudly claimed to be a veteran of the AMC Jeep expedition. His companion, Guillermo, was a tall, muscular black man about half Garrapata's age.

The two were working on a primitive raft, fastening four logs together with cross poles secured by pegs and vines. Their only man-made tools were their machetes which they skillfully wielded. They even drilled the peg holes with their machetes before pounding the pegs in with rocks from the river.

While Garrapata and Guillermo finished their task I calculated wages for the Paya Indians, paying them their eight dollars per day from my precious supply of greenbacks. To conserve my cash, I bargained for an equivalent part of their pay with tools and equipment which I hoped I would no longer need. Tow ropes, my folding shovel and extra water bottles were more valuable to the Cunas than dollars, and they were eager to take whatever surplus gear I could not strap on Amigo.

I also offered to sell two of the watches I had brought along for barter. Eusebio and his mate Mauricio readily traded back part of their salaries for the watches, and I wondered what sort of cultural impact they would have back in Paya where the exact time is of so little consequence. Then I handed Gunga Din my smallest canteen and told him it was a keepsake for his invaluable service to me. I bestowed my machete on Alonso, his father.

Knowing we would soon part, emotions of camaraderie and gratitude toward these gentle people again welled up in me. We bade each other farewell with *abrazos* and the admonition *¡que les vaya bien!* — may everything go well. They left quickly to retrace the trail back to Paya. By nightfall they would cover the same distance that we had agonized through for four days.

Garrapata and Guillermo had finished the raft. The six-foot-long craft looked so primitive that I voiced my concern to Garrapata.

"Do not worry, señor, it will serve us well." he assured me.

I was still skeptical but went ahead and dismantled

Amigo's gas tank and seat. I stored them along with the tank bag and my backpack in the piragua. The three of us then worked Amigo down the sloping bank and onto the bobbing raft, carefully laying the bike on its side. The raft was so narrow that Garrapata had to straddle Amigo's rear wheel to pole the craft out into the river.

I climbed into the piragua. Guillermo poled the canoe from the stern, and I watched the barefooted Garrapata propel the raft. Garrapata appeared competent and I tried to relax. I sat on the motorcycle seat which rested on the floor of the canoe and took in with eyes and camera the river's slowly changing panorama as we drifted quietly downstream.

I was glad to be afloat and not struggling through the dense vegetation lining each side of the bank. Perhaps I could have gotten through by land to the ranger station at Cristales and even to the Atrato, but the odds were rigged heavily in the jungle's favor.

Garrapata had reinforced the warning in the *Backpacker's Guide* that the trail was very rough. I added up the other negatives. I had no Indians to help me and only the light-weight pulley to use on the hills. I was low on gas and food and just about at the edge of exhaustion. I concluded that staying on the land route would very likely end in disaster.

The river had its own risks. Even though the Cacarica was broader than the Tule, it was thick with fallen trees and jungle debris left from the rainy season's flood waters. I could feel the piragua's momentum vary as it responded to currents coursing through narrow channels caused by meanders and rock outcrops.

I spotted white water ahead and kept a nervous eye

on Garrapata, trailing behind as we approached a section of waters rushing between boulders scattered across the stream. Guillermo chose the widest channel and expertly guided the piragua through the gap.

But Garrapata, unable to move the raft with the same precision, poled frantically to follow our course. The awkward craft was slow to respond, and suddenly I saw Garrapata lose his footing on the now-slippery logs and flop over backwards into the water. I watched in horror as the motorcycle slowly slid off the bobbing raft and splashed into the shallow stream, leaving only the tip of a handlebar above water to mark the site of the catastrophe.

I yelled to Guillermo. He reversed the piragua and poled hard toward Garrapata standing chest deep in the water. I jumped into the river to grab the empty raft as it drifted by, almost overturning the piragua.

After anchoring the two vessels we grappled to lift the motorcycle back onto the raft. I was almost in tears as I watched the muddy water running off Amigo and draining from its orifices. I swore mightily at Garrapata. He readily understood the obscenities, even in English, and appeared as contrite as his rough-hewn nature would allow.

We cast off and again floated downriver along a seemingly endless succession of turns and gurgling rapids. Garrapata poled with greater care now, slowing down for the ruffled waters that indicated narrow channels and submerged rocks. But I no longer looked back. If Amigo again slid from the raft, it would suffer no worse damages.

My thoughts were on the future. How could I get

Amigo running again? The nearest BMW mechanic was in a shop in San Jose, Costa Rica — eight hundred miles away. I had a few spare parts in my backpack, but I knew many more would be needed. And repairing the damage caused by the silt-laden river water penetrating Amigo's insides would surely exceed my elementary knowledge of motorcycle mechanics.

"Shit! Shit! Shit!" I cursed as the magnitude of the calamity sunk in.

We floated up to a rough set of wooden steps leading up the riverbank, and I roused myself from my depression. We had reached Cristales, the ranger station where I would have to contact the park authorities.

We tied the piragua and the raft to the stairway and climbed the uneven steps to a clearing at the top. The outpost, carved out of the adjacent jungle, was surprisingly neat. Banana trees and other tropical plants grew around a small grassy knoll. A painted clapboard house with a corrugated metal roof and a wide veranda stood on the knoll facing the river.

Garrapata called hello, but no one answered. We walked around the house but saw no one, and our shouted greetings continued to go unanswered.

"Nobody's here," Guillermo said. "Today is election day, and they have probably gone to Vijao to vote."

Perhaps I would not have to confront the park rangers after all.

"Well let's go to Vijao," I said. "The sooner we get there, the sooner I can start working on the motorcycle."

We helped ourselves to some bananas growing beside the house and returned to river.

Beyond Cristales the terrain grew flatter as we dropped to lower elevations, and the current became placid. The only obstacles to our travel were trees which had fallen across the river. Several times Guillermo and Garrapata jumped into the water to cut away branches with their machetes so the piragua and raft could float beneath the tree trunks.

As dusk was approaching, we began to pass shacks and patches of cultivated land along the banks. In the distance I heard the low rumble of a diesel engine. Guillermo said it was the electric generator at the park office and workshop in Vijao. We rounded two more curves and I saw the generator shed and several buildings on the left bank. We slowly drifted to the opposite bank, at the edge of a nondescript settlement — Vijao.

As we clambered ashore a group of spectators gathered around, noisily gesturing at the sight of our small riverine convoy. The children were especially animated, yelling and pointing at Amigo lying on the raft. For the youngest, Amigo was probably their first sight of any kind of motor vehicle. The village had no roads in or out, and its only communication with the outside world was by way of the river.

We unloaded the piragua and then strained to move the motorcycle from the raft to the landing. Garrapata enlisted several of the more brawny bystanders to help us push Amigo up the slope, where I wheeled it to a halt beside my gear.

Sweating now, and breathing hard from the exertion, I paused to survey the village and its inhabitants who continued to crowd around me and Amigo. So this is Vijao, I thought, glancing at a motley collection of shacks. Loren Upton, who had passed through Vijao on his 1979 expedition, had described the village to me. It appeared even more dismal in real life. God, what a place to be stranded with a drowned bike.

Little did I realize that bringing the disabled motorcycle to Vijao would be the cause of even more misfortune and adversity.

12

Grappling with Gustavo

In trouble, to be troubl'd
Is to have your trouble doubl'd

Daniel Defoe
The Farther Adventures

I sent Garrapata to find a place for me to spend the night, and then I set about reinstalling Amigo's gas tank and seat. As I irritably fended off the inevitable questions from the curious crowd that had encircled me, I noticed a man roughly elbowing his way through the onlookers. Dressed in a clean white shirt and neat trou-

sers, he looked to be about thirty years old, but he projected an air of authority that I immediately distrusted.
The villagers fell back as he stepped up to me, shifting
his stare from me to Amigo and back to me.

"Your papers," he barked without bothering to make
any introductory remarks to establish his position.

I took my passport from the tank bag and passed it
to him. He thumbed through the travel-worn pages, asking the redundant questions I had become accustomed
to at innumerable border crossings and police check-
points.

"Yes, I'm an American....Yes, I have a visa. It's on
page 29."

As I answered politely, the man carefully recorded
the information in a notebook, his only symbol of official
status. Then he turned his attention to Amigo, demanding to see the bike's registration, my drivers license and
the *Carnet des Passages*. He scrutinized each document
and made more entries in his notebook.

"Start the motorcycle and take it to my house over
there." he said flipping his notebook closed and pointing
to the town's largest, least-decrepit building. The house
was only a hundred yards away, but it was just barely
visible in the dusk.

"But the bike won't run," I protested. "It fell into...."

He cut me off angrily and told me to do as he ordered, immediately.

I continued to object, and he suddenly reached for
the ignition key and turned it on. He was about to press
the red starter button, but I quickly grabbed the key and
turned the ignition off.

This son of a bitch knows his motorcycles I thought.

But if he cranks over the engine, compression of the water in the cylinders could easily bend a piston rod. We tussled momentarily as I desperately tried to shift his attention to the water sloshing around inside the headlight nacelle to convince him that Amigo could not run.

"Then push it to my headquarters," he commanded as he turned on his heel and strode off along the riverbank toward the house.

Garrapata, who had returned from his lodging search and had witnessed the encounter, tugged at my arm.

"That man is Gustavo, Vijao's police inspector. He is a mean man and not to be trifled with. They call him *el hijo de puta* — son of a whore. You must do as he says, or he will cause you much trouble."

I finished gathering up my gear and walked Amigo along the muddy footpath toward the inspector's house. I was followed by an animated throng of villagers who had not seen a motor vehicle here since 1979, when the AMC expedition broke through and a few weeks later when Loren Upton brought his jeep in from the other direction.

I was tired, dirty and hungry. I had a tremendous thirst that was getting worse as I continued to sweat out moisture in the still-steamy evening twilight. I was in no mood to joust further with Gustavo, but he was waiting for me on the front porch of the house. The seal of the Republic of Colombia hung from one of the posts supporting the corrugated metal roof. As I wheeled Amigo up to the house, Gustavo snapped his fingers impatiently and pointed to a spot in front of the wooden steps leading to the porch. I parked Amigo there.

Gustavo summoned Garrapata and Guillermo to confirm that I had indeed come through Los Katíos park with the motorcycle. Gustavo then instructed the local head of the park rangers to officially notify me that I had violated Colombian law by introducing a motorized vehicle into a prohibited area.

"You are forbidden to leave Vijao until your case is settled." Gustavo said. "Give me your travel documents and the motorcycle's papers."

I handed Gustavo my passport and the plastic bag that contained the other documents. He arrogantly reinforced his order by reaching over and yanking the key from Amigo's ignition. With a flourish, he dropped it into the plastic bag.

"Report back here in the morning," he snapped. He turned abruptly and walked into the house.

Garrapata said he had arranged for me to stay in a rooming house where I could also get supper. I retrieved my gear from Amigo and left the bike sitting forlornly in front of the inspector's house.

At the rooming house, which turned out to be a run-down hovel, I hungrily downed a meal whose only recognizable components were beans and rice. I shared the "sleeping room" with a half dozen other visitors, but darkness had fallen and I had to use my flashlight to find a vacant corner. I bedded down, without pillow or mattress, on the gaping floorboards.

I didn't get much sleep. The small village never did quiet down, and the other lodgers noisily came and went throughout the night. Once I thought I heard the clang of Amigo's sidestand retracting. I imagined Gustavo out there playing games with the BMW. I should have disabled the ignition system I thought, but I was just too beat to care anymore. Besides, neither Gustavo nor anyone else was likely to inflict more damage on Amigo than the bike had suffered during the last nine days.

Between interludes of sleep I worried that Gustavo had me under virtual arrest, he just didn't have a jail in which to throw me. I didn't think he could send me back. I had a valid visa for entry into Colombia, and Amigo's documents were in order. But he might be able to impound Amigo. I tried to fathom his motives and turned over in my mind what other actions he might take.

When the first slivers of light pierced the cracks in the clapboard walls, I got up and went to the riverbank. I shaved in the debris-filled eddies of the Cacarica and changed into my best pair of jeans, which were as damp and mildewed as my one remaining clean shirt. Back at the rooming house I opened my last can of food — fruit cocktail. I washed it down with a cup of lukewarm coffee I cadged from the señora tending the open-air kitchen.

Well before eight o'clock I arrived at Gustavo's house. I was relieved to see that Amigo had apparently not been further abused during the night. Then Gustavo burst from his front door, dressed only in shorts. He jumped down the steps and angrily rebuked me for being too early. Still yelling, he ran down to the river and belly flopped into the shallow water. Surfacing, he shook himself like a dog, spraying water droplets that glistened in the early sunlight. This must be his morning wake-up routine I thought as I retreated from the house.

Dejected, I took a walk around the squalid village. Vijao consists of about twenty-five shabby shacks scattered around two dirt streets. Although it is the only town of any size west of the Atrato River, this hardly bestows any distinction on the village. I could see absolutely no reason for Vijao's miserable existence. The village has no electricity — the diesel generator apparently serves only the park facilities across the river — and lacks water and sewer systems. Even the *tienda,* the general store, had little to offer, just a few dusty cans of food and some over-ripe fruit. It did not stock the oil and gasoline I desperately needed for Amigo.

My walk around the town only discouraged and depressed me more. I wandered back to Gustavo's office-home, only to find that he had gone to the cantina for breakfast. I made my way to the crude bar and found the inspector sitting on the front porch, drinking a can of beer in company with several other men.

To my surprise, he showed me another side of his mercurial temperament and cheerfully asked me to join him. He was convivial, and as I sat down he invited me to enjoy a beer with him. I thought not, though. I would need all my wits to do battle with him, and a morning beer would not help to balance the odds. My diplomatically phrased refusal did not seem to ruffle him.

Gustavo continued to talk, laugh and joke with his companions, and I could not easily turn the conversation to official matters. After a few minutes, a lull in the conversation gave me an opportunity. As gracefully as I could I asked Gustavo about my status. Instantly, he abandoned his genial manner.

"I am not yet ready to consider your case," he said angrily. "It will be at least a week before I decide how to handle your offense. And if you persist in pressing the matter, it will take even longer!"

I strained mightily to keep my temper in check. I could not win any arguments with this man. He was the only authority here, and he held absolute power. To deal with Gustavo, I would have to draw on reserves of patience I had never before tapped.

I politely disengaged myself from the group and left the cantina. I decided to try to seek out help. I went to see the chief of the park rangers, the man Gustavo had used to press the trespass charge against me. He was apologetic, saying he had only done what the law required him to do.

I told him of my journey through the Darien and asked if he could waive the Los Katíos vehicle ban for the motorcycle.

"You are very brave," he said, trying to pacify me. "But I do not to have the authority. You must bargain with the inspector. It will only make matters worse if I try to intervene on your behalf. Do what he says and pay his price if you want to be released."

So it was back to one-on-one. I returned to the cantina and found Gustavo still drinking beer and in an even more jovial mood. He again offered to buy me a beer, or even something stronger. Then he put his arm around my shoulder and pointed to a piragua beached near the riverbank. Garrapata was curled up in it sleeping off his own drinking bout, fueled no doubt by the wages I had paid him last night.

"See that man over there?" Gustavo said. "He and his companion are going to rob and kill you if you hire them to take you and your motorcycle the rest of the way to the Atrato."

I worked hard to keep from recoiling at the shock of

the accusation, and the unwanted intimacy of the inspector's beery embrace. Garrapata and Guillermo enjoyed the trust of Eusebio and the other Cuna Indians, and that was good enough for me. And if the two had wanted to rob and kill me they could easily have done it when we were in Los Katíos. Nobody would have been the wiser. Why would they wait until my presence was known by the entire village of Vijao and the area's police inspector? But I played along with Gustavo to see where he was leading.

"Really? They would do that?"

"Yes," Gustavo said. "You must have nothing more to do with them."

"But how can I get to the Rio Atrato?"

Gustavo beckoned to one of his companions to join us.

"This is Octavio," he said. "He can take you downriver in his piragua in absolute safety. Talk to him." Gustavo then turned and entered the cantina to get another beer.

Relief swept over me. I might still have a few hurdles to run, but now I knew Gustavo would allow me to leave and to take Amigo with me. And when Octavio introduced himself as Gustavo's cousin, I realized that this stocky, bare-chested man would be my real passport to the world beyond Vijao.

"Okay, Octavio, let's talk business," I said.

But Octavio was shrewd. He knew full well my vulnerable position, and he demanded one hundred dollars for the trip to Travesia, the nearest settlement on the Atrato River. The price was outrageous. The straight-line distance to Travesia less than a dozen miles. I protested and argued, but could only wear him down to ninety dollars. He was probably sticking to his fee because he had to split it with Gustavo. But if ninety dollars freed me from the grasp of Vijao's police inspector, I rationalized, it was actually a bargain.

Octavio said he could leave immediately. I was elated. I retrieved my gear from the rooming house and went to Gustavo's house to get Amigo. I wheeled the bike down to the river and readied it for loading into Octavio's large piragua tied up at the river's edge. Octavio, another passenger and I then wrestled Amigo on board.

I went back to the cantina to report to Gustavo and recover my documents and the key to the motorcycle. But Gustavo ambushed me. His mood had swung in the other direction, and he became irate.

"I am not yet ready to deliberate your case. And for every time you bother me about it, I will postpone the hearing another day!"

Gustavo's outburst shocked me into silence, and I simply shook my head in disbelief. Then I felt a wave of rage rising inside me and forced myself to leave, willing myself not to respond to the inspector. I tramped dejectedly back to the river. I told Octavio that we could not leave. He let loose a string of curses and scrambled up the bank and trotted to the cantina, with me hurrying along beside him. He confronted Gustavo, and their words became so heated I expected the two men to start fighting. Octavio accused Gustavo of being a puppet of the government and a petty tyrant. This set Gustavo off on another tirade, yelling so shrilly and rapidly I could not understand most of what he said.

Octavio retreated, motioning me to follow him. We left the cantina and walked toward the river.

"To argue further with Gustavo is useless," Octavio said. "You will have to sneak out of Vijao after dark. With luck, Gustavo will then let the matter drop and not take further action against you."

"But I can't do that. Gustavo still has the key to the motorcycle. He also has my passport and the motorcycle's *Carnet de Passages*. Without these documents I can't travel further, or even leave Colombia."

"Then you must offer Gustavo money," Octavio said. "Go back to him. Hope that he is willing to bargain, and buy your way out of here."

I returned once again to the cantina, preparing in my mind a series of negotiating offers. Gustavo nodded in reply to my greeting, but did not immediately respond to my request to meet with him in private. Then he stood up and, walking unsteadily, left the cantina and headed toward his house. I followed him, not knowing whether he had agreed to talk with me.

At the house Gustavo motioned me onto the porch and pointed to the rafters. I was startled to see the red hood and door of a jeep resting on the beams. Both displayed the UPTON AND SON EXPEDITIONS insignia. Oh God, I thought, what has happened to Loren Upton and Pat Mercier. How could Gustavo have gotten those parts?

Then I realized they must be from the jeep Upton had abandoned in this area during his 1977 attempt to get through the Darien. The vehicle, almost identical to the jeep he was now using, had bogged down in the swamps and was never recovered.

I asked Gustavo if he had seen Upton recently.

"No, and if *el Flaco*" — the thin one — "comes here again he will suffer a worse fate than you."

Gustavo was probably right. I could not see Upton's temper allowing him to put up with the kind of irrational harassment Gustavo was subjecting me to. Only Pat Mercier's restraining influence would save Loren from an explosive confrontation with this Colombian madman.

Our conversation so far was not creating a favorable mood for a hard bargaining session. But Gustavo had his own means of altering his mood. He unlocked a door to a small office containing a rough wooden desk and two chairs. He opened a padlocked desk drawer and took out a plastic packet of white powder. Using a miniature spoon, he carefully snorted a bit of the powder up each nostril, sneezing and blinking at the effect of the cocaine.

He did not offer me any, which saved me from again having to refuse his "hospitality." He sat silently for a few moments, apparently savoring the euphoria of the drug. Now I knew what accounted for his sniffling and his rapid, often-abrasive personality changes.

"What have you got for me?" he said, abruptly turning his attention back to me.

I started off with the Noriega letter, hoping that revealing my military background and rank and a link to Panama's leader would carry some weight. The inspector carefully examined the document, still damp from the river water that had penetrated its hiding place on Amigo. He tossed the letter back at me.

"You can use that for toilet paper." he said. "Noriega is not the *comandante* here, and I do not take orders from that *pendejo*" — pubic hair — "with the cheeks of a pineapple." Gustavo apparently held the not-uncommon Colombian disdain toward the people of Panama, a country that had once been part of Colombia. And his contempt extended to Panama's strongman with the heavily pock-marked face.

So much for my first try at negotiating. But I noticed a slight softening in his demeanor. Whether it was the cocaine or just the fact that I had a letter from someone in Noriega's position, Gustavo was still receptive and listening.

I showed him fifty dollars and said as diplomatically as I could that I would leave it with him as my "fine" for entering Los Katíos with the motorcycle. He was not moved by my offer, but he did not reject it as I had expected.

"How come you offer me only fifty dollars when you have agreed to pay Octavio almost twice that much to take you to Travesia?" he said. "It should be the other way around. I am the one who has to stay here in this cesspool, while he gets to see the outside world."

"It's all the money I have left," I said, which was close to the truth. I had my travelers checks, but they were worthless here in Vijao. Obviously Gustavo wanted more, so I tried my last gambit.

I took off my wristwatch, the last of the four Swiss quartz analog models, and handed it to him. I told him it was worth far more than fifty dollars. He appeared pleased. He slipped it on his wrist and admired it, probably comparing it to the cheap LCD watches worn by those who could afford such a simple luxury. He asked if it was waterproof, and I shamelessly guaranteed it. I also assured him that should it ever need a replacement battery, he could find one practically anywhere. He continued to look at it approvingly, and I coaxed him into agreeing that it and the money would be an adequate penalty for my transgression.

I held my breath as Gustavo slowly wrote out a note and signed it with a typical Latin flourish. Then he carefully validated it with a worn, almost-illegible official stamp. He passed it to me and I saw that it verified that I had entered Colombia by way of Vijao and had reported to the inspector and been allowed to proceed.

Gustavo gave me back my passport, but when I reached for the plastic packet with the motorcycle documents and key, he stopped me with an airy wave of his hand.

"Más tarde," he said curtly.

Why "later" I wondered. I watched him take another noisy sniff of cocaine before locking the powder and his official stamp away in the desk drawer. He told me to follow him, and he tucked my documents under his arm as we left the office. I walked behind him to the river where Octavio and another passenger were waiting in the loaded piragua.

At the riverbank Gustavo suddenly flipped the plastic bag containing the documents over his shoulder. I had to make a diving catch to retrieve the packet before it fell into the water. Chuckling at my awkward grab, Gustavo asked where my camera was. I told him it was on the piragua and he ordered me to get it. Oh shit, I thought, now he wants that.

I scrambled into the piragua and took my small Rollei 35mm camera from the tank bag. Gustavo directed me to take his picture. I was relieved to learn that was all he wanted, and I didn't mind having a picture of him as a grim souvenir of my humiliation during the last twenty hours. I carefully calculated the camera settings and pressed the shutter release, capturing the smirking Gustavo on film.

I zipped the camera case closed, but Gustavo was no longer smiling. He was shouting and gesturing wildly that he wanted a copy of the photograph. Apparently he assumed I had an instant camera.

But Octavio had already poled the piragua away from the bank, and as the distance between us grew, I became braver.

"You son of a bitch! If my camera had been a gun, your rotten ass would be deader than hell!" I yelled in English.

Relief at escaping from Gustavo's grip flooded over me, and I slumped back on the bottom of the piragua. No longer was I Gustavo's prisoner, but my troubles were not yet behind me. I still had to face the Atrato River basin and get on to Bogotá with a motorcycle that no longer ran.

13

Closing the Gap

...one more river,
There's one more river to cross.

Anonymous Spiritual

I refused to look back as Octavio flung his own last obscenities at Gustavo and Vijao. We fell silent as the piragua slowly drifted downstream. The water flowed steadily but was still too shallow to use the outboard motor, so Octavio poled the long, narrow piragua through seemingly endless loops and bends. The riverbanks were gradually receding, and as we moved into the flatlands of the Atrato River basin they were replaced by swamps on both sides. The river narrowed and became clogged with vegetation. As the jungle growth closed in on us, Octavio had the passenger in the front of the piragua use his machete to give us free passage by cutting away dangling vines and chopping branches off fallen trees.

We drifted up to a fallen tree whose half-submerged trunk was blocking the river. On the far side of the tree, the river had a mini traffic jam. Several piraguas from downstream were waiting while their crews hacked a V-shaped cut into the trunk. The piraguas then slid over the trunk, continuing their journey upriver. After they passed, Octavio navigated our piragua through the obstacle.

The water grew deeper now, and Octavio started the outboard. An hour later we intersected the Rio Perancho, a larger tributary of the Atrato. The water was choked with reeds and water hyacinths so thick the outboard motor repeatedly stalled. Swamps continued to spread out from the narrow river channel, and as far as I could see into the jungle there was no solid ground.

We were now in the area of the proposed route of the Pan American Highway where in 1980 engineers drilled to the limit of their boring rigs and did not locate solid ground. Conventional road-building techniques were not feasible in these swamps. The engineers concluded the road would have to be a high-tech, flotation-type highway that would literally be cushioned on top of the morass surrounding us.

Nothing I had experienced in Africa or Southeast Asia compared with the utter desolation and forbidding nature of this jungle. This is where the real Darien Gap exists, I thought. It is not back in the Panamanian rain forest or even along the steep jungle hills in the Panamanian-Colombian border area. With today's powerful machinery, the Pan Am's road builders could make their huge cuts and fills and easily throw bridges across the ravines and rivers. They could extend the route down to the Vijao area, but then the engineering difficulties would strain modern technology to the utmost.

However it was not the technical challenges that had brought the Darien Gap highway project to a halt. The scheme had fallen victim to a deadly combination of politics, economics and ecological concerns. The United States had lost interest in promoting the highway. Cuts in the federal budget, worries over the spread of Columbia's hoof-and-mouth disease and the Pan Am's perceived impact on the Indian culture had all contributed to eliminating funds for the project.

Without the technical and financial support of the Americans, the other OAS members had little incentive to continue the project, and the Darien Gap sub-committee was slated for elimination. Only Panama and Colombia remained dedicated to the concept — but their capabilities to carry on the work were hardly equal to the staggering task.

The economically crippled Panamanians could not even meet the bills for the new leg from Canglón to Yaviza. The prospect of their extending the route to Palo de las Letras seemed remote. That meant the Colombians, facing their own awesome engineering problems in the Atrato River area, would hardly bring the route to a dead end on the Panamanian border. The likelihood of wheeled vehicles replacing the primitive water craft in the Darien appears to be an unreachable goal.

My thoughts were broken when the river suddenly widened, and I saw huts along the right bank. Octavio rolled on the throttle as we broke out of the thick overhanging vegetation and headed for a wide expanse of water that I knew must be the Atrato River.

We rounded a low-lying headland and turned back to the right, cruising along the edge of the quarter-mile wide river. As Octavio guided the piragua along the shore, I saw a crudely lettered sign: PUERTO LIBRE — PUENTE DE LAS AMERICAS. Whoever had bestowed the title "Freeport — Bridge of the Americas" on this part of the riverbank had been grandly optimistic. I could not relate it to our destination, a collection of buildings that made up the village of Travesia farther along the bank.

Octavio brought the piragua into shore at Travesia, which turned out to be a block-long rank of unpainted shacks facing a narrow dirt sidewalk built along the riverbank. A crowd had already gathered as Octavio and I started to manhandle Amigo ashore with the help of the other passenger and several onlookers. I unloaded the rest of my gear and paid Octavio the ninety dollars we had agreed on. I considered it a reward for his helping me escape from Gustavo.

Octavio pointed out a building with a sign reading: DORMITORIO. I saw the small building not only housed Travesia's version of a hotel, but it also boasted a primitive restaurant and a tiny grocery store. The "dormitory" turned out to be a pleasant surprise. The proprietress showed me a crib-like room so small the bed nearly filled it completely. But it had a mosquito-net canopy plus an almost-clean sheet and a pillow. I readily agreed to the two dollar nightly rate and moved my gear inside.

I had to get to work resuscitating Amigo, and the late-afternoon sun would only be up for a few more hours. My first task was to find engine oil. But I had to look no farther than the store where I found two dust-covered cans of thirty-weight, four-stroke engine oil. I gratefully paid the shopkeeper two dollars for each quart of the precious fluid.

I stripped Amigo of all its detachable parts, drained the oil and discarded the engine's water-soaked air and oil filters. I removed the cylinder head covers and spark plugs, and cranked over the engine with the kick starter, a blessed addition to the G/S model that is no longer found on most large motorcycles. The pistons pumped out squirts of water that spattered on some of the spectators crowding around me, much to their amusement.

"You characters can laugh about it," I groused, "but I'm the guy who has to suffer through all this."

I rummaged through my store of spare parts and found my replacement air and oil filters, battered but still usable. I had to change a bad spark plug wire, and I triumphantly used the extra wire that I should have had last year on the Upton expedition.

As I worked, I cursed my mechanical incompetence and failure to become better qualified in the intricacies of motorcycle ignitions and carburetors. I did as much as I could, but Amigo undoubtedly needed additional work that was well beyond my skills. These repairs, however, would have to wait until I could put the bike into the hands of a talented mechanic in a well-equipped shop.

I finished reassembling Amigo as daylight was fading. I turned over the engine manually, with the ignition off, to let the new oil distribute itself. Then I held my breath and pressed the starter button. I let out a whoop of joy as the engine coughed, caught and sputtered to life in a rough, vibrating cadence that quickly smoothed into the burbling rumble so characteristic of the BMW opposed-cylinder engine.

I let the motor warm up, watching the exhaust emit clouds of steam as the water inside the muffler and exhaust header pipes vaporized. I revved Amigo up and then took a ride along the dirt sidewalk amidst the applause and cheers of the spectators who had supervised my repair job.

Satisfied that Amigo was in reasonably good condition, I parked the bike and headed for the cantina. I celebrated by expansively buying a round of beer for the men on the porch who were peppering me with questions about Amigo and my travels. It was a pleasant interlude. I felt liberated and free after my tribulations with Gustavo in Vijao. Amigo was back up and running. And the beer was cold and tasty, my first since leaving Boca de Cupe, which seemed like months ago. But it had actually been only eight days.

I now had to figure out my next move. The men at the cantina said there were only two conventional directions of travel from Travesia — up or downriver. I could go upriver, heading south on the Atrato by boat toward the river town of Quibdó. This would take me along the route followed in 1961 by the OAS-National Geographic Society expedition's Land Rover. I could then probably find a passable land route to Bogotá.

The downriver option, heading north, was more promising. This was the most-traveled route, and it would take me through the Atrato delta and across the Gulf of Urabá to the port town of Turbo on the Caribbean side of Colombia. Amigo and I could easily board one of the frequent mini-ferries and be transported to Turbo in a matter of hours. There I could find the commercial and official resources I needed — stores, banks and customs and immigration offices.

Turbo was well known to Darien Gappers. The town had served as the staging site for the AMC expedition. Bob Webb and Ron Merrill, along with their Rokons, had boated to Turbo to arrange their transportation back to Panama. And Canadian John Pitt had landed at Turbo in 1975 with his BMW after ferrying his bike around the gap.

Turbo was tempting. It would be so easy to reach. But I didn't want to go to Turbo. And I didn't want to go in the opposite direction to Quibdó, either. Neither town was on the proposed route of the Pan Am. The highway would not run north and south along the river. The plan was to have it run east and west, crossing the Atrato River at "Freeport" on the "Bridge of the Americas."

I went to bed that night pondering the choices. In the morning I found that a good night's sleep had restored my resolve. I had reached Travesia by keeping as close as possible to the Pan Am's tenuous route. British Major John Blashford-Snell had stayed the course on his 1971-72 expedition, and I damned well would too.

I asked around for someone who had a piragua and could get me to Barranquillita, where the Pan Am began again. The hotel owner told me to see Hilario, a young man who had a new, broad-beamed piragua with a reliable outboard motor. I found Hilario working on his outboard just up from the dormitorio.

He said he knew where the road started again and could get me there in his piragua.

"How long will it take?" I asked.

"It's not far," Hilario said. "I can get you there in a couple of hours."

I couldn't help but be skeptical. I wondered if we were talking about passing through the same vegetation-choked swamps that gave the British so much grief. Their expedition had to blast away the vegetation with dynamite and plastic explosives to clear a path for the raft carrying the Range Rover.

But the youthful Hilario's optimism encouraged my confidence in him, and we negotiated a price of forty dollars — almost the last of my carefully hoarded dollars. Then we both set about preparing for our departure as quickly as we could. I was able to buy some food supplies at the store, but I could not get gasoline for Amigo. Travesia's fuel stocks catered to the river traffic, offering only diesel fuel for the launches and premix for the smaller outboards.

Hilario enlisted his two younger brothers to serve as crew members, and they slid the piragua into the river and then hauled a forty-horsepower Evinrude motor to the river's edge. They fitted the motor to the piragua's squared-off stern, and Hilario connected the steering controls and fuel lines.

Meanwhile, I gathered up my gear at the dormitorio and then wheeled Amigo down to the river. Once again I removed the seat and gas tank, carefully storing the tank in the bottom of the boat. The four of us eased Amigo into the piragua, whose wide beam gave it much more room than the more primitive craft I had journeyed on before.

Hilario swung the piragua out into the broad Atrato. He pointed the craft downriver, heading north. He explained we would have to follow the Atrato for about fifteen miles where we would pick up the Rio Tumaradó. This tributary would take us southeast another fifteen miles where we would then turn east to parallel the highway's proposed track.

The going was easy, and I chatted with Hilario. He said he was not a full-time river man but a college student on a financially enforced sabbatical from the university in Medellín. That accounted for his polished manner which had greatly influenced my decision to hire him.

Hilario laughed when I asked if he remembered the British expedition.

"I was far too young to participate in it," he said. "But I remember how the crazy Englishmen came out of the jungle and drank up all the beer within miles. Then they ordered a boat load more shipped upriver from Turbo."

In addition to Blashford-Snell's expedition, Hilario had also heard stories about the AMC Jeep expedition seven years later. But since 1979, no motorized travelers had come through Travesia from either direction. Hilario said that was why Amigo and I had drawn so much attention.

"That sign at the riverbank, the Bridge of the Americas, do you think the Pan American Highway will ever be extended to the Atrato and the bridge built?" I asked.

"That would be very difficult," he said. "Just look around you and see."

From the riverbank out to the low horizon, I could see nothing but the formidable *pantanos,* the swamps that seemed impenetrable even now in the dry season. I shuddered to think what they would be like in a rainy season that lasted most of the year.

We came upon Sautatá on the left bank. It was not really a village but an outpost of buildings for the Los Katíos park rangers. Beyond the hills behind the ranger station was a primitive Katíos Indian village called Unguia. Rumors said the village was the site of a cocaine processing center. As we passed Sautatá we kept close to the far bank.

Several miles beyond Sautatá, Hilario made a sharp turn to the right and we cruised into the Rio Tumaradó which would take us in a meandering southeasterly direction. The Tumaradó's banks were lined with thick jungle undergrowth. Shortly we passed through several small lakes separated by narrow stretches of river — we were crossing the Tumaradó marshes. We emerged into a large lake, a broad expanse of water several miles across that was ringed by low-lying jungle growth. As we crossed the lake a rain shower drenched us with heavy droplets and whipped up the lake's water so that it splashed over the bow.

The squall passed, and Hilario turned the piragua to head due east toward a break in the vegetation where he nosed the craft into a narrow channel. I was concerned. I was tracking our progress with an OAS Pan American Highway project sketch map given to me by

Enrique Ordoñez, a Colombian engineer at the OAS headquarters in Washington. Both the map and my compass seemed to indicate that the exit from the lake was more to the south.

But Hilario threaded the piragua through the rapidly enclosing vegetation, stalling the outboard repeatedly in the thickly matted hyacinths. Finally the channel ended, and Hilario sheepishly admitted a navigational error.

Now we had to turn the piragua around and retrace the channel back to the lake. Hilario's two teen-aged brothers jumped into the shoulder-deep water and used tow ropes to drag the piragua through the beds of weeds. I was reminded of a scene from the movie *The African Queen,* but I hoped the boys would not end up covered with leeches as had Humphrey Bogart.

Back in the lake I pointed to the far southeast corner. Hilario nodded in agreement and steered the piragua toward what appeared to be another opening in the vegetation. Then, off to the right, we saw a large boat crossing the lake and apparently also making for the same opening. The craft, a sport-style cruiser about twenty-three-feet long and with an inboard, stern-drive engine, was moving rapidly and throwing up a foaming bow wave.

The cruiser seemed completely out of place in this desolate area. I asked Hilario the obvious question. And he and his brothers agreed the craft was probably used to run drugs and resupply the cocaine processing centers hidden up and down the river.

We trolled along behind the faster boat and watched as it disappeared into the break in the lake shore vegetation. We followed the cruiser into a broad, well-defined channel that was once again the Rio Tumaradó. We continued to follow the muddy wake churned up by the cruiser. Soon we came to a junction of two waterways, an odd-looking four-way intersection. The wake of muddy water left behind by the other boat indicated it had turned off the Rio Tumaradó and taken the intersecting waterway heading due east.

Both Danny Liska and Enrique Ordoñez had told me of a Colombian project to build a canal to serve as a temporary access to the Atrato River until the highway could be extended from the south. I was convinced that we were at the entrance to that canal. The channel was too straight and the right bank too high above the water to be natural. They had to have been created by a dragline operation, probably a floating rig that had scooped out the channel and piled the muck alongside.

"Let's take it," I called to Hilario, pointing to the branch heading east. The going was easier along this smooth, deserted waterway, and I encouraged Hilario to speed up so we could continue to follow the cruiser. I expected the waterway would bring us into the Rio León at a point not too distant from Barranquillita, where the road started again.

But we never reached the Rio León. The canal suddenly ended at another, smaller, ditch-like branch where we saw the other boat tied up to the bank. Two men were standing in the cruiser, eyeing us suspiciously as Hilario brought the piragua alongside. He asked several questions and the men pointed to the shallow tributary. They talked easily and I heard the word *cuarenta* — forty — several times. I could not understand the context of the word in their conversation, but Hilario seemed satisfied.

He maneuvered the piragua into the tributary, which was so shallow he had to cut the engine. The two boys jumped out and again used tow ropes to propel the boat. I was completely confused now. Where was the Rio León? Then we came to another obviously man-made channel. This waterway was deeper and Hilario started the outboard.

"There it is. There's Cuarenta," Hilario called out after we had gone only a short distance. I was surprised by the sight of several houses up ahead on the left side of the canal. On the right side I saw three oddly shaped hills. According to my map, the three hump-like domes had to be the hills called *Lomas las Aisladas* which were about twenty miles from Barranquillita. The hills were the start of the higher ground that marked the end of the swamps guarding the eastern side of the Atrato River. But best of all, I could see a road just beyond the houses. And it could only lead to Barranquillita!

Hilario explained that Cuarenta was a tiny new settlement located at the end of a new road. Both it and the road were still unknown to cartographers and neither appeared on any map. The Colombians, without fanfare or notice to the outside world, had completed the first phase of their four-phase OAS Darien Gap project to extend the Pan American Highway to the Panamanian border.

Hilario guided the piragua alongside the muddy bank. The four of us slipped and slid as we unloaded Amigo and wrestled the bike up the bank. I attached Amigo's seat and gas tank and nervously started the engine. I was relieved to hear the engine clatter to life and then smooth out as it warmed up.

I hooked on the tank bag and fastened my backpack behind Amigo's seat. Then I brought out my camera to record the moment. I thanked Hilario and his brothers for a memorable trip, for they had helped me accomplish what no one had done before — bring a motorcycle through the Darien along the future route of the Pan American Highway.

It began to rain again as I bade Hilario and his brothers farewell. I mounted Amigo and started out across a field in front of the houses, heading towards the road. I returned the waves of the trio as I passed through an open gate and onto the newly laid gravel track of the latest extension of the Pan American Highway.

It was raining harder, but I didn't care. Because after three years of struggle I had relegated the green hell of the Darien to a minor purgatory. I had done my bit to help Jose March destroy the Myth of the Darien. I had finally closed the Darien Gap.

14

On to Bogotá

*It's a damned long,
dark, boggy, dirty,
dangerous way.*

Oliver Goldsmith
She Stoops to Conquer

I had gotten through the innermost part of the Gap, but I was still a long way from salvation and recuperation. Until I reached Bogotá, I would not have completed Phase Two of my journey along the Pan Am.

So rather than celebrate prematurely, I concentrated on the road. I adjusted my riding cadence to the gravel surface and did not slow to examine the succession of small ranches that lined each side of the road. Obviously, they were newly built, a result of the road now extending out to Cuarenta.

Nineteen miles down the road I came upon a landmark that I recognized — a low concrete bridge across the Rio León. I had never been here, but I recalled the bridge from a photo in Braddon's book *The Hundred Days of Darien*. Major Blashford-Snell had formed up his bedraggled survivors of the Darien brigade and marched them in stiff-upper-lip fashion across the span and into Barranquillita, which was at the time the end of the road coming up from the south.

At Barranquillita the gravel of the new road changed to the pavement of the older road. But the town turned out to be a nondescript village strung out along each side of the highway. There was no gasoline available, so I pressed on toward Guapá. Riding easier now, I was able to open Amigo up and let the bike work off some of the low-speed abuses suffered in the jungle. It was good healing for me, too. I was wet and filthy and suffering a monumental case of travel burnout from the strains of the past weeks. It felt good to be rolling along an open highway.

According to my map, Guapá appeared to be a larger town than Barranquillita. But the map lied — I saw nothing more than a few dilapidated shacks alongside a Y-shaped intersection with the Turbo-Medellín road. I had reached the "Highway to the Sea," which I would have traversed had I gone down the Atrato River to Turbo. I turned right, onto the highway, and pointed Amigo southeast toward the cloud-shrouded mountains that complicated the route to the interior — to Medellín and Bogotá.

In the evening dusk I approached Mutatá, the first town of any size. A customs and police post protected the entrance to the town. I was concerned the authorities might not consider my entry into the country completely legitimate. I had Gustavo's official note affirming that I had entered Colombia through Vijao and had checked in with the police. But Amigo's *Carnet* had not been validated by customs. I was concerned that some petty official might insist that I go to Turbo to have customs officials formally approve my entry into Colombia.

I don't know why, but as I slowed down for the checkpoint the guards motioned me on with a friendly wave, as if my passing was a daily occurrence. I gladly obeyed, still expecting to hear a shout or a whistle commanding me to turn about to face the wrath of authority. But it did not happen.

I located Mutatá's only hotel, where I spent a dismal night, sleeping badly in a dank and mildewed room on a lumpy bed whose thin cotton blanket offered little protection from a night chill I was unaccustomed to. The morning was equally grim. The sky was overcast and I could not find a restaurant open for breakfast. I decided to press on to the next town. After several hours of rough riding over a succession of potholed asphalt and unpaved sections of empty winding road, I found both better weather and decent food in Dabeiba.

The sun broke through the low-lying clouds as I rode into town. I found an attractive restaurant serving a magnificent brunch — hearty soup, chicken stew, rice, bread and steaming, medicinal cups of savory coffee.

The coffee tasted so good I was sure the beans had been handpicked by the industry's television pitchman Juan Valdez himself.

As I was devouring my first good meal in the week since I had enjoyed Lieutenant Miranda's venison steak, a fellow diner overcame his initial reaction to my bedraggled appearance and asked where I was going.

"I'm on my way to Antióquia," I said, mentioning the next major city on the road to Medellín.

"But the road is not open during daytime," the courtly man said. "For the next sixty miles the road winds through the mountains and is in very poor condition, so it is being reconstructed. All traffic is halted between six o'clock in the morning and six in the evening while the work is being performed."

So that's why I had seen so little traffic on the road from Mutatá. This was bad news. I had a long-standing rule against motorcycling at night in Latin America.

"You should rest here until this evening," he said.

The man recommended a nearby *posada* where I could hold up until the highway reopened. The man's suggestion was sensible, but I didn't take his advice. I thanked him and said I would have to see for myself how effective the daytime driving ban really was.

Frustration and impatience began to build in me. What a hell of a way to rebuild a road! Here the Pan Am is the only route in the area and they block it off all day long. I was glad to see that Colombia was diligent in maintaining and rebuilding the highway, but to shut the road down....Well, I'll show them what a motorcycle can do.

I rode out from Dabeiba, up a slight grade and

around a curve and almost crashed into a huge mound of dirt and rocks that a construction crew had thrown up as a temporary roadblock. Beyond the barrier I could see earth movers tearing away at the side of a hill, creating an impassable gap in the roadway.

I asked a workman if there was any way around the construction. At first he shook his head no. But he took a second look at Amigo and pointed down the hill to a river valley. I could see a trail running along the riverbank. It went through a small village and continued on beyond the construction area. The workman said that a motorcycle might be able to get by on the trail.

I turned around and started to work my way down to the river to give the trail a try. But it wasn't so easy. On the other side of the settlement the trail stopped. And a steep, narrow footpath twisting up the hill was the only way to get back on the main road. I parked Amigo and walked the route. I would not be able to ride the bike up the trail. Not only was it steep and full of sharp turns, it was pockmarked with steps that had been cut into the red clay.

I returned to Amigo. By now the motorcycle and I had attracted a crowd from the village. Most were youngsters and I asked one boy to find some rope. Although I had left the Darien, it seems it had not left me — I would have to use the old jungle routine to climb that hill. Within minutes he returned with a coil of stout line. I took the tank bag and backpack off and asked two boys to carry them up the hill. Then I looped the rope around Amigo's front fork and yelled, "Let's go to the top of the hill."

The crowd quickly picked up on the idea, and I soon

had a line of volunteers spread along the rope and pulling Amigo up the path, almost faster than I could scramble alongside and hold the bike upright. Getting around the sharp bends was tricky, and once Amigo and I both fell. But we quickly reached the hilltop, and I repacked my gear onto the bike. I thanked the volunteers for their help.

I mounted Amigo and headed down the road. The going was good for about a dozen miles before I came upon another earthen barrier. Beyond the five-foot high mound of dirt and rock, bulldozers were raising plumes of dust. I could see no detour, so I decided to try dirt biking. I dismounted and kicked a shallow trough through the crest of the barrier. I got back on Amigo and with a running start powered the bike up and over the mound, dragging the underside as I sailed over the crude whoop-de-doo and bounced down onto the road.

The fun lasted only until I drew up to the construction site. High up on the hillside a bulldozer was moving precariously back and forth, pushing avalanches of rock down onto the pavement. Another bulldozer pushed the debris over the side of the road into the valley below.

I sat on Amigo, pondering the situation. Then I noticed the operator on the hillside stop his machine. He waved and pointed to the other earth mover. The Caterpillar on the roadway was crawling toward me, its heavy blade curling a wave of dirt and rock off the asphalt, clearing a path for me. I carefully edged past the clanking bulldozer and waved gratefully to the driver and his friend on the hill, who raised his cap and gave me a vigorous salute.

The road got rougher with more potholes and bumps

as I gained altitude through the steepening *Cordillera Occidental,* the westernmost of the three mountain ranges running through Colombia. It was getting colder. The warm afternoon sun faded rapidly behind dark clouds and then abandoned me completely as clouds of misty rain moved in.

The weather changed so suddenly that I began shivering. I stopped to put on all the rest of my usable clothing and checked the map to see how much farther I could risk riding in the deteriorating weather. My original target, Antióquia, seemed like the only prospect for overnight lodging, so I pushed on despite the chilling dampness.

I worked my way slowly along the mountainous road until I came upon a disheartening sight — another construction area off in the distance, but this one had what seemed to be a mile-long line of trucks, buses and a car or two lined up bumper to bumper. The vehicles were waiting for the six o'clock opening of a temporary roadway that would let them pass through the construction site.

I rode around them to the head of the line. In Latin America, custom allows motorcycles to move to the front of lines of vehicles waiting at one-lane roads, bridges and ferry crossings. At the dirt barrier blocking the road, a flagman refused to let me pass through on my own.

"It's impossible señor," he said. "You must wait here until six o'clock — only an hour more."

My fatigue tempered my impatience, and I shut Amigo down to wait it out. It had stopped raining, but now a stiff breeze whipping across the crest of the hill brought in rolling clouds of silvery mist. I climbed the mound of dirt to look over the construction site as the feeble daylight faded into twilight. I had tried hard to avoid it, but I would be forced into night riding.

I watched the lights of a bulldozer slowly coming towards me. The machine was pushing aside dirt and rock to clear a temporary roadway that would serve for the night. I scrambled back to Amigo as the roaring machine broke through the barrier, shoving the dirt down the side of the hill.

Even before the flagman could signal the line of vehicles to proceed, I took off fast, circling around the bulldozer and sliding through the loose dirt and rocks that were becoming slippery as the mist turned to rain. Raindrops on my helmet face shield blurred my vision, and I flipped it up only to have rain speckle the lenses of my eyeglasses.

This construction area was longer than the others, which probably accounted for the line of waiting traffic behind me. And it also caused the terrifying sight I saw coming toward me — a ponderous line of heavy vehicles slowly grinding ahead and taking up the narrow track's full width.

"Oh shit!" I cried out loud. There was simply no room to pass. With the loose earth and sharp drop-off on each side, the slightest miscalculation or loss of steering would put me over the edge. For once I chose to surrender rather than be bold and foolhardy. I walked the bike over to a narrow shelf of solid ground and watched the lumbering convoy crawl past. I admitted sheepishly that maybe I was supposed to have waited back there by the flagman to let this traffic pass before taking off.

I cautiously worked my way back on the now-deeply rutted and sloppy track, dodging around the stragglers. Suddenly, I thudded up onto solid pavement and realized that I had made it through the construction area. I started down the mountain, slowly feeling my way along the twisting, pot-holed road.

Then Amigo's motor began misfiring, and the bike's mud-spattered headlight grew so dim as to be useless. The day-long slow speeds on top of eleven days of snail-like jungle travel, had not been enough to keep a charge in the battery. I no longer had enough power to activate the ignition circuit.

Practically blind without the headlight, I had to get off the narrow roadway and out of the way of the traffic that would be coming up behind me. I drifted to the right and Amigo bumped off the rim of the asphalt. Both wheels dropped further than I expected. The bike banged down hard against the jagged edge of the pavement and hung suspended by the protruding left cylinder head, crash bar and sidestand.

I eased off the motorcycle on the left side, holding Amigo upright by the handlebar, and fumbled in my pocket for my flashlight. As I shined the bright beam along the bottom of the bike, I was horrified. Amigo was teetering on the brink of nothing! The road had no shoulder, only an abrupt drop-off down the side of the mountain to a valley hundreds of feet below.

I could feel the terror mount as I desperately tried to rock the bike back up onto the pavement. What if I had not been trained to always mount and dismount motorcycles from the left side? If I had tried to put my right foot down first, the bike and I would have toppled over, tumbling down the precipice to certain injury or death for me and destruction for Amigo.

Trembling in fear, I could not wrestle the bike upward. Finally, a truck coming down from the roadblock stopped, and two Colombians helped me lift Amigo back onto the roadway.

I told them what had happened to the bike and asked if I could follow them, using their headlights to guide the way. As I coasted behind the truck, I bump-started the motor and heard Amigo reluctantly come to life. I revved up the engine to try to recharge the battery, but kept the clutch in, staying close behind the slow-moving truck as it inched down the hill in low gear.

On reaching the valley, the road opened up and I was able to upshift. The charging circuit came back on line, and I watched the headlight resume its normal brightness. I pulled around the truck and gave the driver and his passenger a wave of thanks as I cautiously geared up to the fastest speeds of the evening.

The near-disaster on the hill, combined with the cumulative stresses of the day's ride, magnified my weariness. Even so, I began to sense a strange feeling of déjà vu — if only by proxy. I felt as if I was reliving someone else's life. Within the last four days, my motorcycle had fallen into the water and then suffered a lighting system failure on the road to Medellín.

It was eerie because on his trip to South America ten years earlier, nearly identical mishaps had occurred to John Pitt and his BMW, in almost the same places. Here I was, duplicating the misfortunes of the man whose magazine article had inspired me to ride this road. Although John did not take his bike by land through the

Darien, his cycle had fallen into the Gulf of Urabá as he boated around the gap to Turbo. Then he too had been forced into a dangerous night ride and lost his electrics at almost the same place Amigo was blinded.

I dwelled on these coincidences through the scores of dark, twisting miles until I reached the outskirts of Antióquia. It was eleven o'clock and I nervously roamed the dimly lit, deserted streets before finding a pedestrian who directed me to lodging for the night.

At a nondescript motel I had to beg a suspicious night manager to let me into the courtyard to negotiate for a room. I could understand his caution — it was late, and we were in an area notorious for violent incidents, many committed by bandits and assassins on motorcycles. I realized too that my haggard and disheveled appearance added to his doubts.

I convinced him I was a harmless foreign traveler and he finally rented me a room. But he refused to sell me any food or drink. There were no restaurants open within walking distance, so for supper I opened my last can of tuna fish and wolfed it down. Too beat to bother undressing, I crashed on the bed, overwhelmed by an avalanche of exhaustion.

After a mind- and body-jarring cold shower in the gray light of dawn, I packed and roused the wary motel manager to let me out the heavily barred gate. Because of the early hour, the streets were still deserted, but I was lucky enough to find a street kiosk where I could buy a banana and cup of tepid coffee that was so vile it must have been brewed from beans rejected by the export market.

I took off toward the misted line of hills and sharp

curves that led to Medellín, riding along comfortable sections of road that had already been rebuilt. The hour-and-a-half trip was far better than yesterday's trials. Only the biting chill of the higher elevations made the ride nettlesome. My remnants of clothing were no match for the rapid drop in temperature between the valley floor and the mile-high passes through the ranges of the cordillera.

The shivers were combined with a raging impatience to get to Colombia's second largest city. There I could find the sustenance I so desperately needed. Anxious to get on with rehabilitating Amigo and me, I recklessly charged into the city and signed in at the first decent downtown hotel I came upon.

I arranged for a secure parking spot for Amigo. Then it was shopping time. I traded a sheaf of travelers checks for a bundle of pesos and began buying shirts, jeans, underwear and socks to replace the odoriferous, mud-stained tatters that had survived the Darien. I also began a greedy three-day binge of liquid and solid carbohydrates to regain some of those twenty pounds I had lost over the past two weeks.

Another priority was to become legal again. Ever since the Atrato I had been incredibly lucky not to have been stopped for identity checks or inspection of vehicle documents. I sought out the local DAS office — the Colombian internal security department — and put myself at the mercy of an uncommonly sympathetic chief inspector. He listened intently as I related how I had entered the country by way of a solo passage through the Darien.

"Please do not misunderstand me, señor," he said as

he shook his head in wonderment. "I believe you completely, but perhaps you have some proof...."

I had to smile as I dug out my plastic-wrapped papers and produced the primitive *permiso* scratched out by Gustavo, that rear-rank outcast of the DAS.

The inspector read it closely, and I waited patiently for him to ask for further verification, ready to produce my military identification card and to come up with the Noriega letter. But he was satisfied and used up a page in my passport to record his entry. Then he asked to see the motorcycle. I led him out to Amigo, parked on the street a cautious distance from the heavily guarded gate. The battered BMW, still grimy and unwashed, silently confirmed my story of the ordeal. As the inspector surveyed the motorcycle with obvious interest, I raised my other concern.

"How can I get my *Carnet des Passages* form for the motorcycle validated?" I asked.

"Look," he chuckled, "if you got this far on your own, just go on to Bogotá and take care of it at the main customs office."

He gave me a firm, congratulatory handshake and wished me well on the rest of my journey. My pleasant experience with this inspector, a competent, professional police officer in a well-fitted business suit, dampened the lingering bitterness following my encounter with Inspector Gustavo.

The rest of the stay in Medellín served as a desperately needed break in the trip — an antidote for the poisons of the Darien and a healing for the wounds of the ride from Cuarenta. But I still could not remedy my searing travel burnout. A major source of my mental disquiet was the pervasive, drug-inspired wave of law-lessness and violence sweeping the city.

Once, on leaving the hotel, I almost fell victim to the "pigeon drop" swindle. I saw what appeared to be a roll of paper money tumbling along the sidewalk in front of me. A young man who had probably been watching the hotel for likely victims, had tossed the pesos in my path.

"Señor, we are in luck!" he said excitedly, pointing to the wad of bills.

Had I not seen him planting the money, I might have fallen for the con, which would have me putting up an amount of money equal to the "find" to guarantee shar-ing it with my new sidewalk buddy.

But I just grinned at him and said, "Get lost, *pen-dejo,* I'm not your pigeon."

He wasn't offended and even smiled at me. I con-cluded he must have been a clumsy dropout from the infamous Medellín pickpocket school.

During my weekend stay, the newspapers reported twenty-two violent deaths on the city's streets. Four of the victims were policemen.

This tragic, seemingly pointless violence had a per-sonal meaning for me. Many times the street crimes were committed by gunmen riding motorcycles. The po-lice had imposed special regulations for motorcyclists. I could not wear my full-coverage helmet — which could serve as a mask — or ride with a passenger — who could be a machine gun-wielding assassin ready for a ride-by shooting. Some streets were off-limits to bikes, and the police would nervously open fire without asking questions if a motorcyclist, even a foreign traveler like me, inadvertently violated these measures.

So I packed up my new possessions on Amigo and headed further upland to Bogotá. At least, I thought, I would find more reassuring sanctuary there under the blanket of the capital's fortress-like security. I could link up with the Liskas and other friends whom I could call on for help and shelter.

Bogotá would be the penultimate milestone, the goal that Loren Upton had guaranteed me over a year ago. But had I had Regina XI's talent to foresee the future, I would have known that the disastrous events which were to overwhelm me in Bogotá would make Medellín look placid in comparison.

15

Repaying the Darien Debt

There are many people who claim
to have made it through the Darien,
but most of them are liars.

Danny Liska
Bogotá, Colombia, 1986

Bogotá, for all its historic significance and modern-day sophistication, turned into a traumatic way station. Symbolically, it represented the final victory in my three-year campaign to conquer the Darien. But reaching the capital turned into a bitter-sweet success instead of the joyous triumph I thought I had earned.

I had intended for the stopover to be an occasion when I could reunite with the Liskas, kick back and relax and leisurely prepare for my onward travels. But my timing was bad — the Liskas were in Medellín, and had been there during my stay.

So I set up in a hotel and activated the old boy network. The U.S. Defense Attache at the American Embassy, Colonel Jim Coniglio, was a former acquaintance from my Panama days. He offered to let me store Amigo at his residence while I flew back to Panama to exchange my jungle gear for the touring accessories I would need to reinstall on the bike. He also helped book me on a U.S. Air Force C-130 cargo aircraft flying to Howard Air Force Base.

With all the arrangements made, the only thing I had to do was wait a day for my flight. I decided to take a leisurely morning walking tour of downtown Bogotá. For once I was content not to be riding Amigo, so I could work off the effects of the minor malaise I was feeling from the city's eighty-seven-hundred-foot altitude.

As I strolled along a main street, a pleasant-looking, casually dressed man approached me. He was about middle age, but did not have the dark skin and hair of most Colombians. I decided he was not a native.

The man asked if I was a foreigner and said he was, too — a Panamanian and a former Panama Canal Company employee. For proof, he pulled out a voluminous wallet and began showing me various business cards and photos to substantiate his background.

Suddenly someone grasped my arm firmly from behind and said, "Gentlemen, excuse me please."

I turned to see a well-dressed man in a coat and tie.

He had a neatly trimmed moustache and lightly tinted glasses. He looked to be in his mid-thirties, and he reinforced his self-assured manner by introducing himself as Inspector Ocampo of the Bogotá Police Department. He reached into his inside coat pocket, with a flourish that allowed me to see an automatic pistol nestled in a shoulder holster, and pulled out a leather case with a small, embossed gold badge and police identification card, complete with color photo.

"I am a member of the special anti-narcotics bureau," he said. "I have been observing you both and suspect that you are engaging in negotiations for drugs."

Dumbfounded, I began to protest, but he cut me off.

"You are an American, no?"

I nodded. The other man told him he was a Panamanian.

"And both of you carry large amounts of travelers checks in dollars, do you not?"

I admitted I did.

"You fit the profile of foreign drug buyers, and I must consider you both suspects."

Well, hell! Just what I needed, to be busted falsely on drug charges. And in Colombia of all places.

But the inspector held out some hope. "If you gentlemen will allow me to register the numbers of your travelers checks, then you will not be detained. But, if your money is used in any illegal transactions, you will be arrested immediately."

A wave of relief swept over me. If this was all I had to do to extricate myself, then the inspector could damned well scribble away. I quickly agreed.

"Let us then go into the restaurant on the corner and

have a cup of our magnificent coffee while I perform my official duties," he said.

The three of us sat down at a table. The Panamanian produced a folder of travelers checks, and the inspector noted the serial numbers in his leather-bound notebook.

He then recorded my name, passport number, hotel address and room number in the notebook. I took out my eight hundred and forty dollars in checks from the money belt under my shirt and handed them to the inspector. The Panamanian invited me to the counter to get coffee as the policeman began listing my check numbers. We chatted as we waited for service.

"The inspector is a very tough man," he said. "He has been known to shoot it out with drug dealers who do not cooperate with him."

Immediately I wondered how the Panamanian knew about the inspector. Maybe this guy *had* approached me on the street to set up a drug deal. I was becoming concerned. I paid for the coffee and turned to go back to the table. The inspector was not there.

"He's probably gone to the rest room. Maybe you'd better check to make sure," the Panamanian said.

I went to the rear of the restaurant, but the dark, foul-smelling cubicle was empty. Alarmed now, I rushed back to the counter only to find the Panamanian gone too. I asked the cashier about the men, and she said both had hurriedly left the restaurant. I felt sick as I realized I had been scammed.

I ran outside, but I knew my travelers checks and the two con men were long gone by now. I milled about aimlessly, looking for the thieves and for genuine police help. And all the while I berated myself for being taken in by the pair. Losing the checks was much less painful than the embarrassment I felt. Here I was, the Old Pro, Mister Experience, being taken in broad daylight on a downtown street by a couple of artful thieves.

I went to the police station and spent the rest of the day trying to get a bored and contemptuous clerk to make out an official report. By the time I could replace the checks the next morning, I had missed my Air Force flight. So I made a reservation on a commercial aircraft leaving for Panama that afternoon.

I loaded my jungle equipment into a taxi and set out for El Doráo Airport. Around my right wrist I had looped the drawstring of a small nylon bag holding the nine rolls of color slide film I had taken while in the Darien. I carried them separately so as not to expose the film to the baggage inspection machine's X rays. I paid the cab driver and entered the terminal to check in.

As I sorted out my gear I discovered that the small bag containing the color slide film was missing. I dug frantically through my equipment looking for it. Then I remembered I had taken the drawstring off my wrist to reach for my wallet to pay the cab driver. The bag must have slipped unnoticed to the floor of the taxi. I hurried to the entrance, but the cab had long since departed to disappear among the thousands of other Bogotá taxis.

The loss of the film was devastating. I could never replace it. I had lost the more than three hundred photographs that documented my Darien Gap expedition. These were the slides that would graphically illustrate to publishers and readers the stories of the most arduous adventure of my life.

I postponed my return to Panama and spent the next

two days trying to recover the bag. I offered a generous reward, taking out a two hundred dollar advertisement on the front page of *El Tiempo*, Bogotá's leading newspaper. I also placed spot announcements on Radio Caracol and made the reward known at El Dorado Airport.

But nothing worked. I could not recover the film. I surmised that the taxi's next passenger found the bag and took it without telling the driver. When the person found that the plastic canisters contained only exposed film of no value to anyone but me, they were probably thrown away.

I finally abandoned the search and flew back to Panama. At the Road Knights club I switched gear, putting into storage what remained of my jungle equipment and picking up Amigo's windshield, saddlebag, turn signals and the other accessories I had stripped off before venturing into the Darien Gap.

I used my time in Panama to check on events in the Darien. John Mercier said his wife and Loren Upton were marooned in the Colombian wilderness well short of the Atrato River. Two broken axles and a bent drive shaft had immobilized Upton's jeep. The route south from Palo de las Letras that they had taken to avoid traveling through Los Katíos proved to be far worse than Loren had expected.

At the club I met a German motorcyclist who had tried to follow my trail into the Darien on his own. He was forced to return to Panama, though, after his feet became badly infected from insect bites and the effects of the constant humidity, sweat and stream crossings. Seeing him hobbling painfully about made me grateful for my daily routine of using dry socks and foot powder.

A Canadian motorcycling couple at the club told me another disturbing story. They had been touring south in company with another Canadian, a young man riding a Honda 650. A week after I had left for the Darien, the trio took off for Yaviza, intending to follow my trail to Colombia. But on the second day out the couple decided to return after finding out how tough the travel was, and how much it would cost to hire Indians to work the trail and pay for piraguas on the rivers.

The other Canadian said he would continue on alone, but he was obviously unprepared for the rigors of the Darien. He was overweight, spoke little Spanish and was short on money. He thought he could pay his way by working as a gold miner or even selling his motorcycle in Colombia.

After hearing my Darien problems, the Canadian couple were worried that the young man would not be able to make it through. But he had not returned to Panama. Other travelers coming north from Colombia had not seen him or heard anything about him. I shared their concern for his fate.

Another visitor, a Frenchman named Dominique da Silva, had ridden a Honda 650 dirt bike down from the United States en route to South America. After hearing my experiences in the Darien and seeing the German cyclist's afflictions, Dominique abandoned his plans to shoot the gap.

I remained in Panama City another day before flying back to Bogotá on a commercial flight. At El Dorado Airport, the Colombian customs inspectors began calculating import taxes when they spotted Amigo's touring accessories. But I escaped paying duty on them when I showed the officials the Medellín DAS inspector's entry in my passport and explained the reason for bringing the equipment from Panama.

There was still no word of my missing film. No one had turned it in to the airport authorities, nor had anyone attempted to claim the rewards I had offered.

My disappointment was tempered slightly by again meeting the Liskas who had returned from Medellín. I spent most of a day with Danny and Regina XI at the sprawling, warehouse-like building that serves as both her political party headquarters and a quasi-religious temple of worship for her devotees. It was one of three metaphysical centers in Colombia where Regina XI displayed her talents as a psychic.

Meeting her again reinforced my impression that she is an imposing woman — vivacious and emanating a self-assurance that belies her humble origins. Her charisma is built on her psychic abilities, and her followers display a respect for her that borders on fanaticism.

I saw the devotion of her supporters when Danny took me on a tour of the massive building. In one room was a sensually life-like marble statue of Regina XI. A long line of her followers marched around it, reverently stroking the smooth white stone with their hands.

As we moved through the building, Danny showed me medical and dental offices, a pharmacy and restaurants with counters and tables crowded with worshippers.

At lunch in their private quarters, Danny and Regina XI explained that she was considering running for president of Colombia. But they were not sure the timing was right. Colombia might not yet be ready for a woman president. Despite her fame and numerous well-placed connections, she faced strong political opponents.

After lunch we went to the cavernous assembly hall where Regina XI was to address her followers. I estimated several thousand of her disciples had filled the auditorium. Regina XI had now changed into a long, flowing white gown. She was a stunning, queen-like figure who held her audience spellbound. I could almost see her magnetism — not the ordinary appeal of a practiced speaker, but captivating and entrancing in an ethereal way. I wondered if Argentina's Evita Peron had had this same kind of enthralling influence over her followers.

Danny tugged on my arm and brought me out of my own admiring trance. We went into his combined office-library, and he began to debrief me on my Darien Gap adventure. Ever since his hemispheric odyssey he had been fascinated with the Darien. Although he had not been able to take his motorcycle through the gap, he walked through it, back when the wilderness extended for two hundred miles and the danger level was far greater than what I faced.

Now he was an authority on the area, a storehouse of knowledge unequaled by other outsiders. He was eager to hear my story and to record my account on tape, yet was cautious in his acceptance of it. He interrogated me closely on the details. "There are many people who claim to have made it through the Darien, but most of them are liars," he said. Loren Upton had made the same remark to me earlier.

So I had to tell him exactly how I had come from Panama. I described the route from Pucuru, the abandoned Corvair and the misspelled border inscription on the monument at Palo de las Letras. I showed him Inspector Gustavo's note and told him of the hassles I had endured in Vijao. I recounted the wording of the sign on the riverbank at Travesia. Then I talked him through the sketch maps I had drawn of the piragua route from the Atrato through the swamps to Cuarenta. He was particularly interested in the new road from Barranquillita. Although he was aware of the project, he had not known that it had been completed. As an unofficial *Darienista,* he was happy to hear that the Darien passage had been made that much easier.

Satisfied by my narrative, he showed me his extensive files on the Darien — a collection of newspaper clippings, magazine articles and books probably unequaled in any library in the world. He also read me portions of his book manuscript, *Two Wheels to Adventure.* In it he describes his ordeal working his way through the Darien at the height of the rainy season.

We then talked about Liska's Curse of the Darien theory. He reminded me that Loren Upton, for whom the Darien has provided enough misfortune to last a lifetime, is also a believer in the curse. Several years ago, Liska and Upton had considered forming an association of Darien aficionados who would exchange information and compile evidence on sinister happenings to travelers venturing into the region.

I told Danny the stories I had heard about the vanished Costa Rican mule rider and the missing Canadian motorcyclist. And I again expressed my skepticism about a curse.

"But Danny, there are many other cases of people

who have made it through without disappearing or dying. Look at the Brits and the AMC expedition. And look at me. I made it through all right."

"Ah, but Ed, did you really?" he persisted. "Your bike fell into a river, you were arrested, you came close to riding to your death in the mountains, you have been robbed and now you have lost all your film of the journey. Don't you think that's the curse working on you?"

Danny's patient reasoning jolted my non-superstitious, highly pragmatic mind-set, and I had to reluctantly admit that perhaps he was right. Maybe there *was* a Curse of the Darien. He continued his argument.

"Ed, when we first met back in Florida, Regina told me that she sensed you would survive the Darien — that you would eventually get through as you intended. She was right of course. But that does not mean that by succeeding, you have built up an immunity to the curse."

Subdued by his remarks, I bade farewell to Danny and Regina XI and went on to prepare for the road to the south. I continued to ponder Danny's warning, hoping that I had now escaped the curse. I wanted to believe that with my recent misfortunes I had paid in full for defying the Darien.

What I did not know was that time and distance were not defenses. Like a contract with the devil, there would be more installments due on the Darien debt, payable at locations even more distant from the region than Bogotá.

16

In Search of an Epitaph

Do not be afraid of mistakes, for they must be.
But do not make the biggest mistake of all —
doing nothing with your life.

Loren Upton as quoted by Pat Mercier

Even though I had dealt a mortal blow to the obsession by getting through the gap, I still had the death rattle to listen for. But I would not hear it for months to come. I had to cover the Pan Am's thousands of "easier" miles in South America and then ride on northward to Alaska. And, according to Danny Liska's prophecy, all the while

I would have to dodge the parting shots of the curse.

I fled southwest from Bogotá, down the flanks of the Andes along the Pacific route of the Pan Am through Ecuador and into Peru. Then, eighty miles south of Lima on a bright Easter Sunday morning, Amigo's front wheel bearing self-destructed, bringing me to a crunching, shuddering stop. The breakdown was probably another aftereffect of Amigo's dunking in the Cacarica River. But I also wondered fearfully if it might be the curse exacting another payment.

I flagged down a northbound pickup truck, and the amiable driver, Carlos Bonnelli, offered to transport Amigo and me back to Lima. I had to nearly dismantle the bike so we could lift it up into the truck bed, and we were both sweating heavily by the time Amigo was secured.

Carlos, the owner of a machine shop in a Lima suburb, turned out to be a veritable good samaritan. He reminded me that it was a holiday and offered to store the bike overnight on the truck inside his shop. He dropped me at a nearby hotel and picked me up the next morning to take me and Amigo to a BMW automobile shop.

The manager said the agency didn't normally handle motorcycle repairs, but he arranged for one of the mechanics to replace the wheel bearing. He claimed the man knew all about motorcycles. I had to trust him — there were no other BMW repair facilities around.

The work did not proceed rapidly. I made daily visits to the shop to impatiently check on the rebuilding of the mangled front axle and bearing race and watched as the mechanic performed some minor repairs. Finally, on the fifth day, the mechanic pronounced the bike ready, and I paid an enormous bill to recover Amigo. But it was all in vain. As I rode back to my hotel, the electrical wiring under the gas tank burned out in a terrifying, smoking blaze. Miraculously, I was able to douse the fire and still ride the bike back to the shop. The mechanic now had to splice, patch and replace most of the wiring harness.

My only bright moments in the Peruvian capital came in the company of Richard and Mopsa English, the British motorcycling couple I had met back at the Road Knights club in Panama. They had bypassed the Darien by boat and were leisurely riding south, bound for Chile and a hoped-for entry into Argentina — provided the Argentines were in a forgiving mood after having lost the Falklands war to the United Kingdom.

With the latest damage to Amigo righted, I took off southward again, running fast to make up for the un-planned delays in Lima. I crossed over into northern Chile and rode deeper into the fourteen-hundred-mile-long Atacama Desert, where rainfall is a rarity that hap-pens only once a century or so.

I was hard put to keep boredom at bay along the miles of deserted asphalt. With little traffic and no speed limit or highway police to inhibit me, the tempta-tion to open up Amigo was irresistible. The bike was running well, so I indulged in a burst of absolute speed, watching in fascination as the speedometer indicator needle began bouncing against the arbitrary 85 mph limiting post.

The motorcycle had been a victim of the U.S. government's bureaucratic mindlessness that had de-creed motor vehicle operators must not be encouraged to attain excessive speeds by high-reading dials. "Up yours, Joan Claybrook!" I swore at the former director of the safetycrats, an avowed anti-motorcyclist, and rolled on the throttle to its utmost limit. Amigo had no tachometer, but I knew had there been one I would be running up the revolutions to the red zone. I was intent on seeing just how the speedometer would handle the overload.

I became spellbound. The white needle wedged firmly against the pin, and then began to bend. I began a downhill run and Amigo picked up more speed. The indicator continued to fold up against the pin and then bent at an acute angle as the needle rotated even further beyond the limit.

I backed off the throttle and shamefully said to myself: Now why in the hell did you do that? You've screwed up the speedo for good. And I had — I could no longer read my speed, and the twisted needle would later break off. Not long after that the odometer would also quit working.

The damaged speedometer was not the only price I paid for the capricious surge of speed. At my next fuel stop I discovered another casualty — Amigo's right saddlebag was missing. The tubular metal frame holding the bag had broken, allowing the saddlebag clamp to loosen. The bag had dropped off somewhere along the last 220 miles I had covered so rapidly.

I raged furiously against the Teutonic designers of the fragile hardware, not willing to admit that my excessive speed was the cause.

I quickly refueled and doubled back, but now almost at a walking pace as I scanned the roadway on both sides for the black plastic, suitcase-like bag. I tried to recall a sound or change in Amigo's handling that would have alerted me to the loss, but my speed had been too great and the road too bumpy to notice the mishap when it occurred.

I assumed the velocity would have made the bag bounce and carom off the roadway, so I searched the shoulders and gullies to the sides. What made the hunt more frustrating was a profusion of black volcanic rocks scattered all about. The bag could be hidden anywhere among the millions of ebony-colored igneous boulders, each one looking just like the BMW saddlebag.

For the rest of that day and the next, I searched for the bag. All the while I mentally inventoried the contents, deciding what I would have to replace immediately and what could be put on hold. Once through the desert I would have to buy another rain suit. And I needed toilet articles, but I would have to wait until I got home to replace my dental bridgework which had been in the toilet kit. Paratrooper training had taught me not to jump while carrying or wearing objects that could cause injury on impact, and I adopted the habit to my motorcycling.

The bag also contained valuables that could never be replaced, and they were the true measure of my latest misfortune. As I continued my inventory, the same trauma I felt in Bogotá when I lost the Darien film swept over me. Gone were my personal narratives and journals, the sketch maps I had created and the notes I had collected throughout my Darien experience. Gone too were Inspector Gustavo's *permiso* and the draft manuscripts of the story of my jungle adventure. I had carefully enclosed them all in plastic which I had labelled "The Darien Gap Papers."

I recalled Danny Liska's arguments in Bogotá supporting his belief in the Curse of the Darien. It seemed as though the curse was still penalizing me for my passage through the forbidden gap. Miserably depressed, I continued to wonder just how much longer I would be held liable for the intrusion.

I continued south to Santiago and then turned east, following the main Pan American Highway. I passed under the crest of the Andes via a new tunnel leading into Argentina. Fifty miles short of Mendoza, the first city east of the border, Amigo's electrical system failed again.

I was stranded at dusk on a lonely road, and it was dark before I could signal a truck and persuade the reluctant driver and his passengers to haul Amigo and me to Mendoza. They unloaded us on a dimly lit suburban street where I had to fend for myself. I tried to get the bike running, but the ignition charging circuit was out, and the battery had been completely drained.

A car coming out of a parking lot bathed me in light, and the driver paused to investigate. I explained my predicament and he offered to help.

"Come on back to my office, and we'll see what we can do for you."

He parked his car and led me into a nearby building which turned out to be an ice cream manufacturing plant. He introduced me to several men inside, who, he said with a smile, were the "Mendoza Mafia."

They looked the part — dark, swarthy men with Italian-sounding names — but they quickly dispelled my fears with friendly interest in my travels. They also had me sample one of their products, a *paleta,* an ice cream bar on a stick, which was the first solid food I had had since breakfast.

The men urged me to bring Amigo into the building where I could leave it until the morning. Having no other choice, I wheeled the bike inside. Then my rescuer told me to get my belongings and said he would take me to a downtown hotel. He also promised to have another member of the Mafia, a man he claimed was an expert on BMW motorcycles, meet me the next day. After he dropped me at the hotel, I had serious misgivings. Here I had left Amigo in the hands of complete strangers with nothing more than a promise of help in the morning. I could only hope I would be as fortunate as when Carlos Bonnelli rescued me in Peru. I slept restlessly that night despite my weariness.

I had worried for nothing. Right on time the next morning, the motorcycle mechanic met me at the hotel. He proved to be a most extraordinary man. Tullio Braschi, a few years my senior, arrived on a gleaming BMW R62 motorcycle, which he rode helmetless with his gray hair flowing in the breeze. I admired his beautifully maintained machine — a rare classic dating back to the late 1920s. Then he ordered me aboard the pillion seat.

As we rode to the ice cream plant Tullio told me he was an importer of small machinery. In his younger years he had been a motorcycle racer. At a stoplight he pulled up his pants leg to proudly show me a misshapen shin with a collection of deep scars. He said they were his racing trophies.

When we arrived at the plant Tullio verified that Amigo's electrical system was out of action.

"We'll take the bike to my house where I can fix it," he said.

"Okay," I agreed. "Do you have a truck or trailer?"

"We don't need a truck," he said with a laugh. I offered to get my tow rope from Amigo's tool kit, but he shrugged off the idea.

"You just get on your bike and steer. I'll be your engine," Tullio said.

I was puzzled, but I mounted Amigo and Tullio positioned his motorcycle to my right rear. Then he gently pushed me off, shoving with his left hand against Amigo's rear luggage rack. Giving me commands, he nudged us out into the heavy morning traffic. We picked up speed and I heard Tullio speed-shifting — he couldn't use his handlebar clutch lever while pushing Amigo.

We threaded our way through the busy downtown streets, coasting around the corners, until Tullio announced that we had arrived. We pushed the motorcycles into the small courtyard of his combination home, office and workshop, and Tullio introduced me to his wife and two teen-age sons.

"Now you will leave and go enjoy our beautiful city," he said. "Do not return until after your siesta. By then your beloved Amigo will be running like new."

I protested, but he genially banished me to contentedly wander around the tranquil, tree-lined streets of this city which I had not seen for ten years. Although I had only just met him, I trusted Tullio completely. A man who rode as well as he did and who so obviously appreciated motorcycles would take good care of Amigo.

When I returned in mid-afternoon I found that Tullio and his sons had worked wonders on Amigo. Not only had they fixed the electrical trouble, but they had gone over the entire bike, tuning, adjusting and correcting minor problems. We celebrated by Tullio and his boys taking test rides on Amigo — a pleasure for them in that they had not seen this model BMW before. It was the only reward they would accept for their work.

I did not realize it at the time, but this chance meeting with Tullio was another odd coincidence which stretched across the years. Had I not had the electrical failure and been left on the street corner where the businessman found me, I would never have met Tullio — the same man who had befriended both John Pitt and Danny Liska during their motorcycle ventures in Argentina. Pitt had met Braschi during the eight months he spent in Mendoza after his ride to Cape Horn. Liska and Tullio encountered each other while Danny worked on the movie *Taras Bulba* in the Pampas region north of the city.

Leaving Mendoza, I continued eastward toward the Atlantic side of Argentina and the other break in the main Pan American Highway route — the Rio de la Plata separating Buenos Aires from Uruguay. But unlike the Darien, this gap is easily closed by the daily evening ferry which carried me across the broad river to Uruguay and the road heading northeast into Brazil.

The change in direction took me away from the chill of the approaching winter of the southern latitudes. The weather grew warmer on the pleasant route up the coast to Sao Paulo, but then the ride became tense along the dangerous traffic gauntlet of Highway 116 leading to Rio de Janeiro. Before reaching the city, I stopped to pay homage at the imposing monument that recognizes the builders of this part of the Pan American Highway. The towering stone obelisk, which sits on a ridge, is the only tribute to the road system's creators that I have ever seen on the Pan Am.

After a fruitless search in Rio for the Girl from Ipanema and spare parts for Amigo, I struck out on the newest segment of the Pan Am in South America — the seven-hundred-mile uphill ride to Brasilia. The new Brazilian capital, inaugurated in 1960, had grown out of a barren upland plain as the key element of a plan to stimulate the development of the interior of the huge country.

When I reached Brasilia I was at the end of the Pan Am in Brazil. I had almost completed the entire Pan Am circuit between the major capital cities of South America. I needed only to travel the short route between Caracas, Venezuela, and Bogotá to finish this phase of the journey. But how to get to Caracas? There were over sixteen hundred miles of tropical Amazonian wilderness separating me from Venezuela. My maps showed roads of varying quality into the region, leading to Manaus on the Amazon River and north to Venezuela. Full of bravado brought on by my Darien experience, I decided to challenge those squiggly lines on the map that pointed northwest from Brasilia into the interior.

It did not take long for the roads to take on an indefinite character that matched the maps. Beyond Porto Velho, 180 miles short of the Amazon River and the haven of the port city of Manaus, I was halted by unseasonably late monsoon-like rains, which had all but destroyed the roadway, washed away the rickety wooden bridges, and stopped the cable-guided ferries.

I surrendered to the weather, reasoning that this route wasn't a part of the Pan Am, so I could cheat without remorse. I retreated to Porto Velho, and arranged for an expensive overflight of the Amazon to Manaus for me and a crated-up Amigo.

The road north of the river was not much better. It took another ten days to work my way through the desolate Indian country. Unlike the Darien Indians, the Brazilian tribes are far more aggressive in opposing encroachment from the outside. On one stretch, called "the hundred kilometers of nothing," army troops at a roadside checkpoint advised me to hurry through the area lest I make an easy target for Indian blowguns and arrows.

The ride along the reddish slash through the northern Amazon rain forest was unnerving and solitary. The road alternated between rutted, dusty tracks and axle-deep mud. Once I was trapped out beyond sunset on a deserted road, halted by a broken motorcycle frame mount. It was fully dark by the time I completed emergency repairs. I imagined all sorts of dangers about to overtake me from the jungle — but the only threat was from the swarms of insects attracted by my gamy sweat and the feeble light of my pocket flashlight.

I worked my way north to Caracarai and then to the new city of Boa Vista where I had to wait for a visa to enter Venezuela. Then it was across the border to Santa Elena, and on into the Gran Sabana region. I was glad to make the crossing into Venezuela, to end my struggle with Brazil's Portuguese language and the abominable gasahol that had Amigo's engine pinging in protest. Now I could converse intelligibly in Spanish, and the bike reveled on its new diet of octane-rich, heavily leaded gasoline.

South of El Dorado the terribly rutted road turned to asphalt and became an absolute joy after the hundreds of miles of rattling, frame-breaking corduroy road. I ran quickly on to the Orinoco River and crossed on the ferry at Ciudad Guayana. From there I dashed across the lowlands to the Caribbean coast and Caracas.

I spent only two days in the capital, anxious to cover the remainder of the Pan American Highway leading back to Bogotá. The first leg went well. It was not until I entered Colombia that I ran into another one of those Pan Am anomalies. Heretofore I had been faithfully tracking along the broad red stripe on the American Automobile Association map of South America that defined the main route. At Pamplona I continued due south on Route 71, but became dismayed when the road, now twisting up into the cloud-shrouded mountains, turned to gravel, then dirt and finally a narrow, single track.

How could this be I wondered. Both the locals and the few road signs I saw confirmed that I was on the right route to Duitama and Tunja, but I could not believe that this was really the Pan American Highway. Yet it was. Despite the far better road from Pamplona to Bucaramanga, the Colombians had designated this abominable trail as the official route, most likely to garner OAS and U.S. credits to eventually improve it. That tactic had worked before, but it meant more painfully slow, cold, wet riding for me and constant abuse for

Amigo. The road back to Bogotá had turned into the back road to Bogotá.

When I reached the capital, I allowed myself only two days there, and the stay was not enjoyable. At every turn I seemed to be reminded of my previous misfortunes. Even a brief visit with Danny Liska was depressing. He was wearing a cast on his right arm — a souvenir he said of an assassination attempt on Regina XI. The brake lines on her Mercedes had been cut in Medellín, apparently by political opponents. But Regina was in another car when Danny, driving the sabotaged Mercedes, careened wildly down a hill and crashed. Danny commented wryly, "They play pretty rough down here."

I did not consider for even one fleeting moment the possibility of returning to the Darien for a northward passage. The rainy season was in full swing, and I had already had my adventure of a lifetime. Now all I wanted to do was put paid to the curse and get back to the United States as fast and safely as Amigo could carry me.

Luckily, I was able to arrange for a gypsy cargo aircraft to ferry Amigo back to Panama. But the luck turned into a near calamity. Just before departure, the Colombian authorities impounded the plane. They suspected it was being used to smuggle narcotics.

I was already booked on a scheduled passenger flight, so I had to leave for Panama not knowing when Amigo would follow. While waiting for the motorcycle to arrive, I visited friends and caught up on the latest Darien news.

Loren Upton had abandoned his disabled jeep short

of the Atrato River, and he and Pat Mercier had broken
out of the jungle on mules and on foot. They went to the
United States, determined to return again next year to
repair the jeep and push on to the Atrato River and
beyond.

At the Road Knights I learned that no other long-
distance motorcyclists had ventured into the Darien,
going either north or south. Unfortunately, there was
still no word of the missing Canadian biker who had
followed me into the gap.

Five days after I flew into Panama, Amigo arrived,
and I took off up the Pan Am. I didn't dally along the
way. I was suffering a severe case of travel burnout, the
worst I can remember. Amigo and I made a reckless,
headlong flight back through Central America and Mexico to the international bridge at Laredo to complete the
third phase of my journey. I had reached the spot where
my Pan Am adventure had started more than three
months earlier. Or had it really begun twelve years ago
on my first BMW, which I rode from Washington to Panama? Or even before that, on my first trip along the Pan
Am with my daughters in the old, lumbering
Volkswagen?

Whatever the actual starting date and place, I had
almost put the obsession to rest. All I had to do now was
travel the main Pan Am in the United States and Canada. But I steered Amigo to the east, back to Florida, to
rest and regroup for the final assault on the Pan Am the
following summer.

It was a good move. I was able to leisurely prepare
for the last lap in my hemispheric journey. In June 1987
I rode back to Texas and followed the northwest track of

the original route of the Pan Am in the United States. I paralleled the Rio Grande to El Paso and then swung north along the high plains east of the Rockies to Wyoming. There the highway turns northwest, through Montana to Sweetgrass and the Canadian border where it crosses into Alberta.

The ride was a motorcyclist's dream. Amigo, completely refurbished, effortlessly covered the miles of almost endless prairies, and easily sped through the hills and curves of the Rockies. I experienced a sense of release never before possible on my entire journey. No longer did I have to wallow through the cultural quagmires of Latin American money, language and customs.

Best of all, I was not traveling alone. The road to Alaska was crowded with vacationing travelers — long lines of lumbering recreational vehicles, and a heavy mix of motorcycles. It was easy to form up loose convoys of bikers, sharing the roads, campsites and north woods scenery. I was having a sedate fun run, which belied the knowledge that this road carried the same name as the far more challenging Pan American Highway passages in Latin America.

Only after crossing over into British Columbia and reaching Dawson Creek did the mystique of the road to the north appear. I was now venturing onto the Alaska Highway — as full of historical consequence as any segment of the Pan Am to the south.

Known first as the Alcan Highway, this eighteen-hundred-mile road between Dawson Creek, British Columbia, and Fairbanks, Alaska, was a product of World War II. Within the frantic summer of 1942, the quickly mobilized battalions of U.S. Army engineers and civilian contractors cut through the nearly impassable muskeg and permafrost of the north woods. They created an improvised land resupply route to Alaska, then under attack by the Japanese in the remote Aleutian Islands chain.

As I rode along the hard-packed gravel tracks, which were interspersed by newer, straighter sections of asphalt, I could not help but compare the engineering challenges faced by the World War II road builders with the obstacles of the Darien Gap highway project. If they could build the Alaska Highway under such handicaps, what about the Darien? The difference, I concluded, was that there was no wartime emergency or patriotic enthusiasm to justify permanently closing the Darien Gap. To revive the Darien project and forge the last link in the world's longest highway would take a multi-national obsession of hemispheric proportions.

But for me, I was coming to terms with the force that had driven me for so long. I had conquered the gap, and all the miles on each side of the Darien. It was time to celebrate. Fittingly, I rode into Fairbanks, Alaska, on the Fourth of July 1987, and I converted the holiday to my own private celebration for having reached the end of the road. It was a day of personal independence for me — I silently declared the obsession dead.

Epilogue

¡Amigo Vive!
BMW Motorcycle Owners of America *News*

The quiet demise of the obsession did not end my involvement with the Pan American Highway. Nor has it isolated me from the other adventurers who have been caught up in the lure of the road and the Darien.

Loren Upton, still driven by his desire to complete his world-girdling journey, refused to let the Darien beat him. In 1987 he and Pat Mercier returned to Colombia and located the abandoned jeep. They repaired it, and on the 741st day since we had first rafted across the Chucunaque River at Yaviza, they crossed the Atrato River, 125 miles to the east. They drove on triumphantly to intersect with the Pan American Highway.

They continued on to the road's end in Argentina, on Tierra del Fuego, and then sailed with the jeep by boat from Chile to South Africa. There they began another grueling hemispheric adventure, taking two years to work their way north.

They suffered incredible hardships—malaria, dysentery and a score of broken springs and axles on the jeep. Once, in the Sudan, they had to abandon the vehicle and devise a raft from the jeep's interior parts to float down the Nile River to find civilization, help and food.

After surviving their African ordeal, they traveled in stages through the Middle East and Europe and arrived at Gamvik, Norway, on July 4, 1989. It had taken Loren Upton fourteen years to reach the north Cape since his first departure from Alaska. His feat, now shared most deservedly with Pat, is an absolutely courageous achievement that assures him a place in the ranks of his immortal heroes of centuries ago. Loren and Pat are now caretakers of a ranch in Salmon, Idaho. They have begun another formidable challenge—distilling Loren's voluminous daily journals into a narrative that will reflect the true magnitude of their determination.

In Colombia, Danny Liska has published his book *Two Wheels to Adventure,* and Regina XI has continued her political-religious ministry. She ran for the presidency of Colombia in 1990, failing at the polls but not losing her life as did two other candidates in that violence-marred election.

She continued her role as spiritual advisor to General Noriega almost up to the time of the Christmas 1989 U.S. invasion of Panama. Even though the General was wearing red underwear on the advice of Regina XI and a gold amulet in her image—which had belonged to Danny before Regina XI passed it on to Noriega—their alleged protective qualities were rubbed off when Noriega surrendered to face drug charges in the United States. Noriega was convicted and is serving a 40-year sentence in the Federal Correctional Facility in Miami, Florida.

In September 1994 I had a meeting with the U.S. Army Lieutenant General Marc Cisneros, who was in charge of the U.S. Army forces in Panama at the time of the invasion. He was the key figure in arranging for Noriega's capture as a "prisoner of war." General Cisneros confirmed Noriega's belief in witchcraft and knew of the Panamanian's wardrobe of red underwear, but until meeting with me, was not aware of the connection between Noriega and Regina XI.

In 1992 Regina XI was elected to the Colombian National Senate, where, according to Danny Liska, she "was like a loose cannon." Her luck also ran out on October 15, 1994, when she was kidnapped by so-called Marxist guerrillas from her ranch near Cali, about 180 miles southwest of Bogotá. According to press reports, the guerrillas told Regina's daughter they would release her mother later with a message for the government regarding its offer to negotiate a peace agreement.

Liska himself has been waging a desperate battle against the ravages of ill health, which have included leukemia, an enlarged spleen and heart palpitations. He is recovering slowly, but at only 160 pounds he hardly resembles his previous bearlike stature.

The Canadian John Pitt, now in his mid-80s, survived a near-fatal accident when he fell through the ice on a frozen lake and was trapped for hours until rescued. Almost dead from exposure, he suffered an out-of-body experience. He said, "I was floating about five feet above the lake in a sort of ethereal form, quite comfortable and warm." He called the incident a preview of life after death. Although he has recovered, the lack of oxygen to his brain has caused memory loss, and he can no longer manage the BMW motorcycle he used on his 1975 ride to Cape Horn.

Richard and Mopsa English, the British motorcycling couple, went on to successfully complete their ninety-thousand-mile journey. Their fascinating book, *Full Circle Around the World with a Motorcycle and Sidecar,* tells of their four-and-a-half-year adventure which took them through sixty countries.

The Darien Gap still continues to attract adventurous travelers. In 1988 a young Norwegian motorcyclist, Helge Pedersen, became the first biker to come though the gap from the south. Pedersen, on a world tour on a BMW R80 G/S identical to *Amigo,* came upriver by boat and canoe from Turbo to the Los Katíos park ranger station at Cristales. With the help of a German backpacker and two native guides, he fought his way by land to Palo de las Letras and on to Paya, Pucuru and the other way stations to Panama City. But he paid a terrible physical price. He suffered a broken hand, broken and cracked ribs and a badly infected foot which laid him up for a month and a half at the Road Knights club.

I had heard about the tall, bearded Norwegian from gossip on the road. Once in Guatemala we passed each other but were unable to stop and share our experiences. I finally met him at a motorcycle rally in Pennsylvania in 1989, and Helge told me the full story of his Darien experience. "Ed," he said, "if I had known what you had gone through I would never have tried to do it. And now that I have survived, I would never, ever try it again."

I watched fascinated as Helge narrated a color slide show of his inter-continental travels. His presentation brought to mind haunting memories of the same locations in the Darien where I had composed almost identical photographs—the pictures that were on the rolls of film I had lost in Bogotá. After our encounter, Pedersen continued his round-the-world travels and has also written a book on his adventures.

In the 1991 dry season, a Brazilian became the third motorcyclist known to have negotiated the gap. Antonio Braga, a businessman now living in Oaxaca, Mexico, returned to his former home in Brazil by riding his 1990 BMW R100 G/S. He followed generally the same north-south route that I did except for using piraguas to get to Paya. He spent six days on the overland route and then used the Rio Cacarica and the Atrato River to reach Turbo. Here he was delayed for almost a month getting clearances for himself and his motorcycle.

I met Braga in Oaxaca in 1993. He showed me his photo album, and I was able to identify landmarks along his route and spotted in his crew two of the Indians who had helped me. We agreed the experience was unforgettable but not to be repeated.

The Darien region remains as dangerous as ever. A 1994 Associated Press wire story described it as a place where "there are swamps that can swallow a man. Packs of wild boar have devoured unwary travelers. Some travelers get lost and go mad. An Austrian was found naked on a trail, crazed by panic, hunger and clouds of insects."

Even though the gap has been shortened (tending to reduce the physical challenge of the route), the per-mile risk from human predators has risen sharply. Ironically, it has taken centuries to moderate the hostility to outsiders of the Cuna, Choco, Emberas and Katíos Indians, but the indigenous population is being overwhelmed by an invasion of *maleantes* who endanger natives and passers-by alike. The indiscriminate victimizers are the drug traffickers, illegal immigrants, gold-seeking grave robbers and, more recently, heavily armed Colombian bandits and kidnappers, often masquerading as revolutionaries.

Incidents of random violence on the Colombia side include the kidnapping two years ago of a Dutch tourist from his room at the park headquarters. He has not been seen since. More recently a Danish trekker was found murdered on the trail.

On the Panama side, a group of Colombian invaders raided the village of Pucuru on January 31, 1993. After looting the village, the raiders took three of the resident New Tribes missionaries back across the border, holding them hostage and demanding $5 million for their release. (One of them was Richard Mankins who helped me on my 1986 passage.) The status of the missionaries remains in doubt. A faint radio transmission heard on December 15, 1993 renewed hope for their survival, but the resolute New Tribes Mission stands against paying any ransom, leaving the kidnappers with little incentive to free their captives.

Adding gravity to the incident is a rumor that the missionaries were suspected of reporting the presence of a nearby jungle drug-producing operation, probably the 220-acre coca field and cocaine processing site discovered by rescue teams searching for the captives. The boldness of the raiders has forced the New Tribes Mission group to close its operation in Pucuru and to withdraw all other representatives in the Darien region.

As for the gap itself, it remains as a 67-mile break in the Pan American Highway. Although there was a well-publicized meeting between Panamanian and Colombian officials which revived interest in the project, nothing concrete has been forthcoming. In a visit to the Darien in 1991, I found the road to Yaviza was almost impassable. In Colombia, Danny Liska reports "there is no hope that this road will be built. Colombia has trouble keeping up the roads it now has, and landslides are forever blocking passage. Guerrillas are in control of all the hinterland, including the Choco."

As for me, I continued to ride my faithful *Amigo*. The bike and I have now logged over 257,000 miles together. I did, however, have to arrange for an engine transplant to rid the motorcycle of the Darien's lingering effects. In a carefully planned rehabilitation operation, several of my very talented cycling cohorts rejuvenated *Amigo* by replacing the old, worn-out engine—which still carried remnants of the Cacarica River mud inside. In 1994 *Amigo* was inducted into the

American Motorcyclist Association Motorcycle Heritage Museum in Columbus, Ohio, as part of a display of "adventure touring" machines.

In the years following completion of the trip to Alaska, I continued to make periodic return trips to Panama. Five of those runs were leading motorcycle tours through Central America. These trips have piled up the Pan American Highway miles to the point where I have exceeded Danny Liska's record for two-wheeled travel along the Pan Am.

My perspective of the Curse of the Darien has undergone a recent change. Seven years ago, after my triumph, I balanced off Danny Liska's belief in the threat with the astute remark of another friend— Ed Friedman of Balboa, Panama. Ed has his own evaluation of the curse. "The Curse of the Darien is nothing more than a self-fulfilling prophecy," he said. "High-risk people, like you, doing risky things are bound to invite disaster far more often than us more conventional folks."

Ed's assessment is loaded with logic, but recent events have forced me to reassess the curse. First, Danny Liska was plagued with a variety of medical problems, and in 1993 I was diagnosed as having Amyotrophic Lateral Sclerosis, more commonly known as Lou Gehrig's disease, which ended my 500,000-plus-miles riding career. But I have no regrets and can look back more rationally on my Pan Am run with its Darien adventure, seeing it as a youthful wish that started in Washington and later developed a dynamic life of its own.

But what's wrong with that? Malcolm Forbes, the late publisher and motorcycle enthusiast, believed that daydreams are doable and that anything you haven't done is an adventure. He advised, "Don't stay put when you can put your foot into any part of this still whole, wide and mostly wonderful world."

Ed Culberson
The Army Residence Community
San Antonio, TX
November 1994

Publisher's Note
Lou Gehrig's Disease took Ed Culberson's life on Jan. 4, 1995.
Danny Liska died of leukemia on May 9, 1995.

Index

Conclusion

When Memory Fades

This bike, an '81 BMW R80 G/S, feels as old and tired as I do. The huge tank is battered and touched up with paint that is laughably mismatched. A thick rubber band circles the instrument cluster, squeezing everything together. Cracked saddlebags let in the rain. It is a five-stroke engine, the last one being Faith.

I am taking this bike on its last ride. Of a half-million or more BMWs produced in seventy years, few are more famous than this one. *Amigo* is painted on the sides of the tank. What was once bold color is now pastel and fading, as paint will do after 267,000 miles. But in twelve brutal days in February 1986 this motorcycle slogged out of a jungle and into immortality.

Its owner, Ed Culberson, is a legend in BMW circles. A retired military officer, Peace Corps MSF instructor, explorer, and writer, he is also the kindest, most gracious man one could meet. But privately, in his younger days, he was by his own admission, obsessed. He wanted to ride *Amigo* the length of the Pan-American Highway, from Alaska to the bottom of South America, including the nearly impenetrable jungle between Panama and Colombia—the infamous Darien Gap.

The stretch from the Yukon to Panama was easy. But the road stopped there. Culberson stared at a green wall to the south. His first assault on the Darien ended in failure. The following year, when the rains abated in early 1986, he made it, pushing the bike through a sixty-seven mile path he cut with a machete, canoeing across rivers, and ultimately emerging in Colombia after nearly two weeks of unimaginable hardship. Then he continued south until the road stopped again. He stood in Tierra del Fuego; to the south, across the Straits of Magellan, lay Antarctica.

It had taken two years, but *Amigo* was the first vehicle ever to have traveled the Western Hemisphere nearly from pole to pole. The incredible story of triumph over monumentally adverse conditions is related in Culberson's 1991 book, *Obsessions Die Hard.*

Now Ed himself is dying. The hand that throttled a motorcycle through jungle mud is weak, the victim of Lou Gehrig's disease. He will never sit on his bike again. I volunteer to take it from Ed's home in Florida to the Rider Rally in Richmond, Kentucky. There a BMW company transport truck will take it to Westerville, Ohio. It is going into the AMA museum, to sit for a year with its equals. Few are.

I tell Ed what an honor it is to ride his bike as he hands me the key. Some last photos are taken. His daughter helps him into the car and we wave goodbye. He and his bike, together for so long and through so much, part. I ride north.

This poor motor will look out of place in the sea of gleaming Wings with their winking lights and neon glow on the rally grounds of Richmond. An ocean of Armor All will never clean the bike; the jungle did its work well and permanently. But in the Westerville museum each dent and tinge of rust will be a valorous badge of the highest distinction.

Near Nancy, Kentucky the sun is not cooperating. I want to see it drop below the horizon at the end of a limitless stretch of straight highway. And I want to take a photo with a telephoto lens of the motorcycle heading into that setting sun, to make it look like a yellow basketball a yard from my nose. But this is hilly country, there are late afternoon clouds, and I give up. The picture I never capture of *Amigo* that afternoon still remains as clear to me as any Kodak moment I ever had.

The sun disappears. In the east, a few degrees above the horizon, a full, bright orange moon is rising. It is perfect, this planetary Zen, with one body vanishing and another appearing in a galactic juggling act. Ed is dying, his daughter marries; *Amigo* goes into a museum and another BMW rolls off the Berlin assembly line; now the sky darkens and tomorrow there is light anew.

In time everything will fade, like the paint on the tank. Ed and those of us who had the privilege of knowing him will be no more. Maybe then *Amigo* will be forgotten. But I hope not.

Bob Higdon
November 1994

Bob Higdon is a semi-retired trial lawyer and a freelance writer who rides about 50,000 miles a year on his two BMWs.